Jay —

I hope you enjoy stories — and lessons — from the other side of the looking glass. Some did not learn the lessons!

[signature]
Raven 45

MEETING STEVE CANYON

...AND FLYING WITH THE CIA IN LAOS

By Karl L. Polifka

Raven 45 – 1969

Copyright © 2013 by Karl L. Polifka
All rights reserved.

ISBN: 1-4909-7985-9
ISBN-13: 978-1-4909-7985-4

INTRODUCTION

Steve Canyon was the name of the lead character in a comic strip created by Milton Caniff. It was published from 1947 through 1988 and featured senior Air Force pilot Steve Canyon who went from one exotic adventure to another during the Cold War. Caniff stressed intrigue and unusual adventures and locale in the escapades of his lead character. That was a comic strip. Then there was a bit of real life.

In 1962, in the midst of an evolving war in Southeast Asia, the United States, along with North and South Vietnam, China, the Soviet Union, and others signed a neutrality treaty regarding the Kingdom of Laos. The intent, at least on the part of the United States, was to try to mute the leverage of the Communist forces of North Vietnam in their efforts to dominate South Vietnam, and to help shield an unprepared Thailand. The North Vietnamese immediately violated the neutrality treaty followed by the United States and other signatories. However, United States involvement in Laos was markedly different from that of the North Vietnamese who injected increasing numbers of regular forces into Laos both to create and operate logistics support for their South Vietnam operations in the form of the "Ho Chi Minh trail", and to dominate the somewhat hapless Pathet Lao, the Lao Communist faction, in an effort to conquer Laos.

The United States effort centered on the paramilitary operations of the Central Intelligence Agency, eventually supported by an increasing use of US military air power. The presence and activities of US government personnel, both CIA and military, were publically low key and somewhat unobtrusive in keeping with the spirit of the much violated neutrality treaty. By 1967 the situation required the presence of experienced US Air Force Forward Air Controllers (FAC) to direct the increasing amount of tactical air power supporting CIA and Lao government military operations. These FAC, using the call sign RAVEN, lived at five locations in Laos but their records were maintained at Udorn, Thailand. They flew unmarked airplanes in civilian clothes, without military identification, and at the direction of the US Ambassador to Laos were restricted to small numbers of personnel. This effort, and associated activities, were referred to in the US Air Force as "Project 404".

I arrived in South Vietnam on 28 September 1968 and departed on 28 March 1969 with most of my time spent working with US Army Special Forces in a remote border province. My nearly nine months as a Raven were at Long Tieng, Lima Site (LS) 20A, not far from the Plain of Jars, where I worked for CIA and the Hmong led by General Vang Pao. Every person's experience during the war in Southeast Asia was colored by when and where they were, and what they did. This account is of what I experienced in Southeast Asia on my first tour. For a more complete view of the entire spectrum of events in Laos, I highly recommend the book Shooting at the Moon by Roger Warner. Additionally, Jim Parker provides a case officer's perspective in Code Name Mule and Covert Ops.

A few comments about names are in order. I have, with few exceptions, not used the names of CIA personnel because I do not remember all their names and don't want to offend anyone, and also for implicit

INTRODUCTION

security reasons that, oddly, persist to this day to some extent. The Air Force aircraft maintenance men that I worked with in Vietnam and Laos were universally superb at keeping our planes going in tough conditions. I only name one of them because, again, I don't remember the other names. There are a few names I know but don't use because of some dramatic errors on their part and there is no need to embarrass them further.

Lastly, you will find repeated and well-deserved criticisms of the command structure, direction, and practices of the United States Air Force in Southeast Asia. Their approach to this war was too focused on World War II experience and doctrine, and not on the reality of the situation in much of Southeast Asia. This rigid view led to missed opportunities, wasted resources on a grand scale, and periodic tragedies. This is not implicit criticism of the fighter and attack pilots that we worked in Laos to achieve goals directed by the United States Government. Their performance was usually good and frequently excellent. You should feel free to draw institutional parallels in later operations. Unfortunately, they are not hard to find.

Karl Polifka
Raven 45
1969

DEDICATION

This book is dedicated to the Ravens who did not return
and to
The Central Intelligence Agency and its paramilitary case officers who defined, organized, and ran an operation that created the standard of success in the use of airpower and indigenous forces in the most difficult of circumstances
and to
The Hmong whose population fought a brutal war for fourteen years with resolute courage and dedication but at a terrible cost

GLOSSARY

AAA	Anti-aircraft artillery. Usually thought of as cannon fire. In Northern Laos this included 37mm, and an occasional 57mm in addition to heavy small arms, 12.7 mm (.50 cal), and 14.5 mm
AGL	altitude above ground level
ARVN	Army of the Republic of Vietnam.
CBU	Cluster Bomb Unit. Various versions but most common was CBU 24 whose dive released canister contained 680 bomblets, each about the size of a tennis ball, each containing 250 ball bearings propelled at 4000 feet per second on detonation. About 5% of the bomblets did not explode but are lethal forever.
CIDG	Civilian Irregular Defense Group. The indigenous force at any given USSF A team location. Usually 500 to 700 locals.
G force	Force of gravity. Sitting in a chair is one G.
INFIL/EXFIL	Ground force talk for troop insertion or extraction.
KIAS	Knots indicated airspeed
Knot	One knot is a nautical mile per hour. One nautical mile equals 1.1508 statute miles.

Long Tieng	Pronounced *Long Chen*. Headquarters for General Vang Pao, the CIA, and Ravens for Military Region II in Northern Laos.
LZ	Landing zone.
Maps	1:50000 scale used by ground forces and FAC, displayed as UTM (Universal Transverse Mercator) coordinates.
MIKE	Acronym for Special Forces Mobile Strike Force. Usually 4 US and 500 indigenous troops.
NVA	North Vietnamese Army. Term usually used by Americans. Correct term is PAVN, People's Army of Vietnam.
ORDNANCE	In addition to CBU, the most common ordnance was Mark 82 500pound bombs, Mark 117 750 pound bombs (Mark 82 and 117 came in "Slick" or "high drag" versions). Mark 84 2000 pound bombs, Mark 118 3000 pound bombs, and 500 pound napalm canisters.
PLAIN OF JARS	The Plain of Jars is frequently referred to by the French name of Plaines des Jarres or the abbreviation PDJ. All terms are used here.
RLAF	Royal Lao Air Force. The Hmong portion were referred to as *Cha Pao Kao* roughly translated as "Prince of the White Cliffs". Of the eight T-28 pilots I knew at Long Tieng, one survived.
RPG	Rocket Propelled Grenade. Intended as an anti-tank weapon it could penetrate

	10 inches of armor with its shaped-charge warhead, then incinerating anything in an enclosed interior. It had a minimum shrapnel effect when it airbursted.
STRIKE PATTERN	Generally two types, racetrack and random. The race track was usually at lower altitudes and facilitated shallow dive angles to deliver high drags and napalm but was not good in a high threat area. Random was higher altitude and circular with attacks coming from different directions at different times. Necessary in high threat areas.
TACS	Tactical Air Control System. The joint ground-air system for assigning air assets to specific targets.
DASC	Direct Air Support Center. Regional filter/approval center.
TACP	Tactical Air Control Party. Bottom rung in the TACS strucure.
TASG	Tactical Air Support Group. Parent unit of TASS in SE Asia.
TASS	Tactical Air Support Squadron. The unit having administrative control over those assigned to FAC operations. Five in SE Asia.
USSF	United States Special Forces. US Army Special Forces.
VNAF	South Vietnamese Air Force

Thanks

My thanks go to my lovely wife Lois who has had to endure
these and many other stories for over 35 years.
And to
Roger Warner who sent me the cover photo and
for all his expertise on a difficult subject.

CHAPTER ONE

It was my third night there, another quiet evening spent talking to my new roommate, Don Zlotky. We were Forward Air Controllers (FAC) sharing our single O-1F "Birddog" and attached to Advisory Team 32 at Gia Nghia (gee-ah knee-ah), the capitol of what was then Quang Duc Province in South Vietnam. Our Fort Apache compound was due west of Cam Ranh Bay and near the Cambodian border. There were about 75 Americans in the advisory team, seven of which were US Air Force members including our Air Liaison Officer (ALO), Major Frank Hilbush, the third pilot.

Our room was one of six in an old French single story building that housed Advisory Team officers, and undoubtedly the French 20 years before. It had a central latrine and heavy wooden shutters over the screened no-glass window openings. The plaster walls held the eternal traces of the red highland dust, kept to a minimum by the daily Montagnard maids. The lights in our room consisted of a 25 watt desk lamp and a small fluorescent ceiling fixture. It was certainly enough light to see the expression on Don's face suddenly change as we both heard dull swishing sound outside. He knew what the sound was, I didn't.

Don started moving in what seemed like slow motion and told me to follow since I had yet to be assigned to one of the 13 bunkers ringing the compound. He didn't need to tell me to bring my CAR-15 (Combat Assault Rifle 15, a short barreled version of the M-16 with a telescoping stock) and the 300 rounds in my bandolier. My steel helmet and flak jacket were still enroute but that was a minor concern at the moment. He whacked the lights off and ran into the night while I followed closely as we thumped across the compound, intersecting the shadows of others pounding towards their positions. A siren was wailing in the dim moonlight when I discovered the origin of the swishing sound.

A rocket propelled grenade (RPG) whistled directly behind me, leaving a fiery trail before detonating against a building. There were sporadic dull booms and flashes as incoming mortar rounds exploded. In an instant we approached a waist high stone wall left by the French. I skipped the steps and made it in one jump, learning what adrenaline can do for you. We tumbled into Don's position – the "alternate command post". Actually, it was a slightly glorified foxhole with enough radios to substitute for the heavily sand-bagged command post, should it get flattened. Mortar rounds and RPG continued slashing into the compound at a leisurely pace. Our own two 81mm mortars started returning fire accompanied by the four 105mm howitzers of an ARVN battery slightly above us. The machine guns in our bunkers remained silent – there was nothing to see to shoot at in the darkness.

The bad guys stopped firing after 15 or 20 minutes, as did we. We remained in position for about an hour in case there were any surprises and then the Advisory Team 32 commander and Province Senior Advisor, Army Lt. Colonel Metcalf, directed us to stand down. The score for the night was several dozen 82mm incoming mortar rounds and a smaller number of RPG. No casualties on our side and little damage. This would become a near weekly routine, sometimes with heavier incoming fire.

CHAPTER ONE

That night, like the ones before and the ones after, was punctuated every hour for five minutes, beginning at 55 past the hour, by the harassment and interdiction (H&I) fire of the four guns of the ARVN 105mm battery. Within a few nights it was a routine that I did not hear. It was an interesting phenomenon that any incoming fire awakened me instantly, while I slept through the outgoing. This was common I was told. I was assigned to a bunker the next day, a short 70 feet or so from our room.

The O-1 was a conventional landing gear ("tail dragger") built starting in the early fifties by Cessna. It was a good, tough, airplane that could work from forward areas and be maintained there. It was not a short takeoff and landing (STOL) airplane but it could work fairly short dirt strips which the newer USAF FAC airplanes, the Cessna O-2 and North American OV-10, could not. The Air Force had acquired the newer airplanes at least partly, they said, because of the O-1 lack of speed – it cruising at about 85 knots (100 mph). It was really more of a matter of *being there* rather than *getting there*. Being near the battlefield, however defined, gives one a situational sense that does not come through in messages or phone conversations.

The O-1 – we had the F model with a variable pitch prop – had two seats in tandem with large side windows forward on either side of the pilot. The forward windows were opened with a latch from inside the aircraft and popped up, locking into a clip on the under-wing surface. The rear windows, considerably smaller, could be opened inwards and clipped in place. The Forward Air Control mission required three radios -- an FM for contact with ground troops; a VHF for contact with the local base radio operator and some aircraft; and an old 12 channel crystal UHF set for use with fighters. The UHF was a disgrace which the USAF would not replace because "it would cost too much", and "other (new) sets would not fit the existing cabling and rack". A Special Forces MIKE (Mobile Strike) Force pooled some money and bought their USAF O-1 FAC a tunable Wilcox UHF that fit the rack and cabling just fine. They switched back to the antique before Air Force maintenance inspections. The problems with the old crystal set was that you couldn't monitor "guard" (243.0) UHF emergency frequency at the same time you were on another channel, you had a limited number of preset frequencies, and if a crystal burned out during a strike you were left without options.

The O-1 had a 213 horsepower Continental O-470 engine that consumed about 9 or 10 gallons an hour out of two 20 gallon wing tanks. It normally cruised at 85 knots and had superb visibility. Any O-1 pilot will tell you he loved the airplane for the visibility and because it was tough. It did have, however, some significant shortcomings. The attitude indicator and heading indicator were old vacuum driven instruments that were not terribly reliable. The cockpit instrument lighting was a couple of strange small ultra-violet lamps that showed you what you were looking at in the darkness of night – sort of. Lastly, forward visibility in rain was very poor.

Getting into the O-1 and getting it going was a skill acquired fairly quickly. You put your left foot on the fuselage step and your right hand on the windshield brace. Then you pulled yourself upward into the front seat with your right hand, a move that required a quick duck-and-swivel. There was no parachute to get in the way, so that made things easier. The cockpit smelled like old zinc chromate, engine oil, and sweat that oozed from the ancient olive drab seat cushions -- the only fabric in the airplane. The door emergency jettison handle near your right knee was a nearly a custom-made place to park a CAR-15 with its telescoped stock, and a bandoleer with 15 magazines.

After strapping in, set the throttle to idle, mixture rich, prop full increase, and then flip on the battery, generator, and fuel pump switches on the electrical panel near your left elbow. The fuel pump whined nasally as pressure built to the normal range. Let it sit there for a second or two, turn it off and push the engine start button. After a few swings of the prop, and a little jockeying of the throttle, the engine coughs to life. The radios will warm up by the time you make a quick scan of the few engine instruments and the crew chief has pulled the chocks. Running the engine lean is a good idea if you are stuck with a long taxi or prolonged idle operation. A few hundred feet into the take-off roll, a little forward stick pressure brings the tail up, and a little back pressure lifts the airplane off a few seconds later. Assuming an unwarped frame, the O-1 will climb at around 600 feet per minute (fpm) with the normal load of a pilot and eight white phosphorus (Willie Pete or WP) marking rockets.

Air Force air crew at that time were issued one piece cotton flight suits that were a medium gray (there were some olive drab ones) and got lighter in color after a few washings. One would have to be a bit crazy to think about evading in the jungle wearing this gray neon sign. Most FAC wore the standard issue jungle fatigues or Special Forces "tiger stripe" fatigues if you could get them (we could). "Fatigues" are now called BDU – battle dress utility.

Don spent a couple of days in our O-1 backseat checking me out in Quang Duc Province. This included landing at three Special Forces A team sites we supported and being introduced to our main customers. Quang Duc covered about 2500 square miles and had a population of perhaps 30,000, most of them Montagnards. The three A teams were at Duc Lap, very near Nam Lyr mountain in Cambodia; Bu Prang to the northwest of Gia Nghia and near the border; and Nhon Co some five miles to the north of Gia Nghia. A sizable portion of the northeast part of the province had trees spaced far enough apart so that the ground was easy to see. We rarely patrolled there. A good chunk of the southeast part of the province was what was called the "sea of bamboo". The bamboo was so thick that it was nowhere possible to see the ground, or follow terrain features. There was a major north-south trail there and included, we were told by Montagnards, bamboo woven into interior archways or cave-like passages that assured safe transit of the large numbers of North Vietnamese regulars that flowed past constantly. Patrolling there was pointless and no friendly ground operations operated there. We were, in essence, a small island in a moving river of NVA regulars and supplies.

There were two remnants of the French colonial past that caught my attention. The first was a magnificent plantation house in the northwestern part of the province not far from Bu Prang. The house was large, had a blue tile roof, and at some time in the past must have been a magnificent place for the plantation owner and his family. Now it was pretty much of a wreck sitting in the tan grass of the low hills. I couldn't help but imagine what it must have been like to live there, an uneasy and unhappy local populace nearby, the wind moaning in the lonely night, with an edge of fear in the wind. A second landmark was a means of dealing with any uncooperative members of that native population. At the intersection of Route 8 and Route 13 in the midst of a wilderness was a gallows platform that looked like it could handle four hangings at a time.

Our compound, perhaps six acres, was a small fortress. Each of the 13 bunkers had a machine gun, two of them .50 caliber. The bunkers were large holes in the ground with probably three feet of sandbag walls several feet thick, supporting a sandbagged roof. Five or six people could fit into one. There were 22 coils of razor wire in two stacks encircling the compound. Scattered around the inner perimeter were 280 electrically detonated Claymore mines. The two 81mm mortars and the ARVN

CHAPTER ONE

105mm battery were the offensive firepower. Additionally, within the compound were CS (riot control) gas canisters that, theory had it, would flood the compound with incapacitating gas should we be overrun. We were supposed to carry gas masks during an attack so that if the canisters were used we could fight the bad guys hand-to-hand. No one bothered to carry gas masks.

In addition to our Air Force O-1 there were three Army O-1 and three Army pilots. There was little artillery for them to adjust so they spent most of their time observing the province, as did we, and providing position reporting to any Special Forces operations that requested it. The airfield, created when Army engineers pushed two small hills together, was 60 feet wide and 2000 feet long and elevated perhaps 75 feet above the town of some 3000 people. By this time I had a grand total of 64 hours in the O-1 so I had a lot to learn. At this point it would be useful to describe what a Forward Air Controller (FAC) was supposed to do.

A good FAC (and there were bad FACs, just like there were bad fighter pilots) had a lot of things to do. Assess the weather (since there was no weather reporting), observe friendly and enemy activity, coordinate and plan with friendly forces face-to-face and via radio, keep track of friendly positions, respond to requests for airpower, control the use of airpower pass-by-pass, report results of airpower use as accurately as possible, and intervene as necessary and to the extent possible when things went bad. The FAC also needed to understand the strengths and weaknesses of the various fighter and attack units, be knowledgeable of the effects of various weapons, and maintain situational awareness. All this might sometimes involve the use of all three radios in the O-1 – UHF for fighters, VHF for the home radio operator, and FM for the ground troops. As situations got tense, and later they would be ultra-tense all the time, the toughest job was staying cool.

MEETING STEVE CANYON

In Vietnam FACs were a part of what was called the Tactical Air Control Party or TACP. Our little contingent at Gia Nghia was a TACP and was at the bottom of a decision-making pyramid called the Tactical Air Control System that involved the Air Force and ground units and their hierarchy. If the immediate application of airpower was requested for, say, troops-in-contact (TIC) or a fleeting high value target, a request was made by radio to the next layer up the chain. This would be the regional Direct Air Support Center (DASC) and, simultaneously, the next level up on the ground force side. If they had no objection they remained silent as the request went to the Tactical Air Control Center (TACC) at 7th Air Force headquarters in Saigon – with a call sign of BLUE CHIP. The TACC, depending on aircraft availability and priorities would then task a fighter/attack unit to respond to the request. While this may sound cumbersome, the whole process normally took less than a few minutes. Since there were always fighters on alert, we could expect them to arrive at the stated rendezvous (a navigational fix) within 15 to 20 minutes of our request. What is described above was referred to as an "immediate". The other side of the coin was what was called a "pre-plan" – a target selected by 7th Air Force and the use of attack assets pre-planned by them. The significant problems associated with pre-plans will be described later but served to highlight severe shortcomings in experience, perspectives, and attitudes by those in charge.

Life at Gia Nghia quickly set into a routine, albeit one in which there were periodic surprises that were learning experiences, among other terms that could be used. Our flying time was restricted to six hours per day on the aircraft, except for emergencies, since universal unrestricted flying would overwhelm the 21st TASS (tactical air support squadron) maintenance operations at Nha Trang on the coast where 100 hour inspections occurred. Since we had one airplane, and since we flew it

CHAPTER ONE

about 180 hours a month, taking it to Nha Trang involved something of an airplane shuffle so that there was always a FAC aircraft available at Gia Nghia. Should there not be, we were authorized to commandeer an Army O-1 in a tactical emergency.

Don and I flew about 80 hours a month each while Frank flew the rest. He had over 10,000 hours in the C-124 and didn't need or want the time. On a normal day one of us, after the usual good breakfast, would drive our jeep to the airfield, less than a mile across town where our two maintenance guys would have the O-1 ready to go. A usual day involved flying along at 1500 feet above ground level (AGL), cruising at 85 knots, and trying to observe abnormalities that might indicate enemy movement or presence. Checking in with one or more of the Special Forces A teams might provide some clues as to where to look in a lot of triple canopy jungle that was interspersed with naturally clear areas that we called "the golf course".

Landing at one of the A teams locations and talking things over added additional insights. Checking in with any on-going A team operations in the field was also routine, as was giving them a position check. In my first few days I was flying along an old and unused road left over from the French days. Two things caught my eye. The first was some road construction equipment left from those days, including a steamroller. That makes one think a bit. The second item was more impressive. A tiger was walking down the road, heard the noise of my O-1, looked up and snarled while pawing at the air. That made for another quick engine instrument scan! That area used to be a place where the big time game hunters, including Teddy Roosevelt, came to hunt tigers. I rather doubt that there are any left now.

Don and I did a lot of position checks on deployed SF operations. These normally consisted of two Americans and a hundred Montagnards. The normal procedure was for the SF guy to radio that my engine noise was, say, south of him. I'd fly north in his general direction. He'd keep making corrections until I flew directly over him and he would call it. I'd roll to where I could see the point where he was under a mass of jungle and then fly away a few kilometers and figure out on the 1:50000 exactly where that was. Circling around him would indicate to the NVA where he was located, so that was a no-no. When I had figured out his location I would radio it to him using a pre-arranged form of code. I was usually accurate to within a hundred meters. This, obviously, was many years before GPS.

Another periodic chore was to check SKYSPOT locations. 7th Air Force, as part of their pre-planned operations, would have a radar station direct a fighter to a point where the radar site would command ordnance release in order to hit, it was hoped, some area deemed worthy. This was called SKYSPOT. We were supposed to observe the intended drop point and then locate evidence of every piece of ordnance released and assess damage, if any. This was made more difficult by map survey inaccuracies in our area. I learned two things from this exercise. One was that F-100 pilots seemed to disdain the whole process and were not very accurate while B-57 crews were excellent. The second was that there was almost never anything to report in terms of "damage", calling into question the process by which these "targets" were selected.

The daily routine consisted of flying and observing as described above and then sitting around the compound reading, writing letters, or staring at the ceiling. I found that Joseph Heller's novel, Catch 22, made a lot more sense in my current environment. The food, furnished by the Army and cooked by hired Vietnamese, was pretty good. Our rooms were cleaned by Montagnard "maids" at a very modest rate, and clothes washed but rather roughly. Every 90 days each man got a "sundry pack"

CHAPTER ONE

(or one pack for 90 men for one day) that consisted of ten cartons of mostly cheap cigarettes, a bunch of cheap pipe tobacco, various other items and, somewhat oddly, 36 bars of Ivory soap. If one person used all that soap in the shower in 90 days they might well be considered rather compulsive. We gave the surplus soap to the maids who were utterly delighted, given the qualities of Vietnamese soap.

Our "officer's club", about the size of a couple of a largish residential dining rooms was open from five to seven – heavy drinking not being a good idea. It was dimly lit and had wood paneled walls and was the scene of some interesting conversations and stories. The bartender was a pretty local Vietnamese young woman who was referred to as Co Phouc – meaning "Miss Phouc". Her last name caused occasional lewd comments. This was usually followed by a film which was different every night. Lt Colonel Metcalf had assigned the chore of finding and transporting movies to the Army O-1 pilots. It being the highlands, it wasn't too hot compared to sea level temperatures. Not bad, really, except that it was boring until it was time to run an airstrike or experience the periodic mortar attack.

My first break in this routine came after I'd been there a week when I worked SHARKBAIT, two F-4C from Cam Ranh Air Base (AB), on a pre-plan target. The standard F-4 load in South Vietnam was six Mark 82 500 pound "slicks", or six Mark 117 750 pound "high drags" on each airplane. A "high drag" had fins that popped out after release slowing the descent and, with practice, providing more accuracy than slicks. The downside of high drags was that the delivery speed had to be slower with a shallower dive angle. This would not be good in a high threat area. The Air Force, later, employed high drags in high threat areas with predictable results.

I worked Sharkbait in a racetrack pattern, as we did all flights in Quang Duc at the time. A racetrack pattern is just that, an elliptical circuit

MEETING STEVE CANYON

around which the two fighters "ran". The FAC stayed close to the friendlies so that it was obvious, hopefully, to the fighters where they should not drop ordnance. Our dialogue went something like this:

"Walt two-one (21) (my callsign), Sharkbait on two-three-six-decimal six (236.6)"

"Sharkbait, Walt 21 confirm rendezvous at two-four-zero at four-zero off PYRAMID , and say line up". (40 miles on the 240 degree radial from Pyramid, the TACAN navigation station at Ban Me Thout).

"Roger on the 240 at 40 off Pyramid. Sharkbait is two Fox four with 12 Mark 82 slicks".

"Sharkbait, Walt 21, target is a suspected supply site, elevation two thousand two hundred, weather clear, wind north at five, expect small arms fire, instantaneous fusing and release singles if possible" (which would give more coverage of an ill-defined target). "We'll do a racetrack west to east, I'll hold on the south side. Am in the target area now".

"Walt 21, Sharkbait copies instantaneous and singles, copy two"?

"Roger", Sharkbait two replied.

"Sharkbait coming up on the rendezvous".

The O-1 didn't have a TACAN (Tactical Air Navigation beacon) receiver but looking at a map I know about where 240/40 was. Looking up I can see two F-4 approaching in a descent. It looks like they are leveling at about ten thousand feet.

"Okay Sharkbait, Walt 21 is at your ten o'clock low, rocking my wings" The O-1, painted a flat gray, stood out against the heavy green jungle below.

"Sharkbait has a tally" (a derivation of the British tally-ho) we're turning west for a run to the east.

"Roger, Walt 21 is in to mark." I pull up, throttle to idle, and roll left until the nose is well down and the target area centers on my windscreen.

CHAPTER ONE

My left hand reaches up and arms one rocket and I pull the trigger. The 2.75" diameter rocket with a 28 pound white phosphorus war head blasts out of its tube, supersonic in a couple of seconds. I turn left as I climb, seeing lead nearing a roll in position, keep him in sight, check the smoke, and make my call. "Lead, 100 meters west of my smoke, got you in sight, cleared hot".

Lead replies, "lead's in hot". He is in a steep dive, adjusting as he picks up speed, a couple of minor turn adjustments and a single bomb departs the green and tan camouflaged F-4. The bomb streaks towards the jungle like a dark pencil line in the sky as lead arcs up and to the left, back into the racetrack. The bomb blossoms orange and darkish gray as 500 pounds of explosive and steel rip through the deep green jungle. He actually did hit about a hundred meters west of my smoke. Things won't always work that way.

I have two in sight and make the call. "Two, make yours about 200 meters east of lead, the other side of the mark – cleared hot". He acknowledges and releases. The bomb plows through the trees and erupts in fury.

And so it goes, pass by pass twelve times until they call "Winchester" (out of ordnance) and join up high over the area while I orbit around the ripped jungle at 1500 feet trying to find any signs of damage to anything. This is called "bomb damage assessment" or BDA. In a case like this the BDA would be "a hundred over a hundred, NVR smoke and foliage" which translates to 100 percent of the ordnance was within 100 meters of the target, no visual results due to smoke and foliage. Sharkbait and I both know that this is a bunch of trees and there was unlikely to be anything there. They headed back to Cam Ranh Bay and I switched over to VHF and pass the BDA to our radio operator, CARBON OUTLAW 69. He would pass it along to the DASC, just so the reporting correlates, which it sometimes did not.

MEETING STEVE CANYON

This was the first unsupervised airstrike I had directed. Granted, it was simple and in perfect circumstances, and very easy. I would think about any implications later. The O-1 rumbled along for another hour or so as I observed and reflected on whether I had done my job correctly, and how I could do better. Circumstances, I would find, would guide that direction and outcome.

I hadn't been at Gia Nghia long before I was standing outside one evening watching our mortar crew get ready to do some H&I fire (I was later to discover how inaccurate they were). It was another form of entertainment. One member of the mortar crew was a mental category 4 case.

Robert McNamera, Secretary of Defense, had forced the Services to accept 100,000 of those defined as mental category 4 – otherwise ineligible for military service due to a severe intelligence deficiency. The Army wound up with way too many of these guys. This individual at Gia Nghia had, before my time, been assigned to man the entry gate on guard duty. This was a small compound with a small gate – which was closed at 1900 (7 PM) every night. Slightly to the rear of the gate, on both sides, were a total of four Claymore mines focused on a kill zone in front of the gate. A Claymore looks sort of like a large but thin book and has some 700 pellets driven by a C4 plastic explosive charge. When detonated the force of the charge forms the pellets into .22 caliber size projectiles that rip out at 4000 feet per second for an effective range of about a 100 meters.

They checked the guy out on the gate. "... If someone drives up at night, an unlikely event, turn on the lights. Here is the light switch (click up and down) to see who they are. If it is the NVA, very unlikely, you plug in the Claymores – pushing two connectors together (which is certainly not like a light switch) ..." It seems pretty simple, doesn't it? One night he was on duty when one of the USAID (US Agency for International Development) guys drove up to the gate after it was closed. Mr. Mental Category 4 really did mean to turn on the light switch, but he plugged in the Claymores. Four Claymores sent 2800 .22 sized pellets screaming into the kill zone where the jeep was stopped. It was an utter miracle, I was told, that the USAID guy was not pulverized. The jeep was turned into a pile of shredded scrap metal and the USAID guy, sitting at the wheel, went into a total mental breakdown. They removed number 4 from the guard detail.

They did put him on the mortar crew in a simple job. One does wonder what he did when the mortar crew was not working, which was frequently the case. If you've seen film of a mortar crew working there is a guy who lifts the round to the lip of the mortar tube on the command "hang it". On the command "fire", issued about a second later, he drops the fat end of the round down the tube and bends down for another round. The mortar is then triggered and the round fires. Forty G of force arms the set-back fuse. Hanging it was the job for #4. That night as I was watching, #4 was doing just fine hanging it. Thirty, forty, perhaps fifty rounds and then he tried to put the pointy end down the tube. That would have resulted in the tube having to be lifted up, it is not light, and the round shaken out. Fortunately, the mortar pit boss saw what #4 was about to do and grabbed the fat end before the round went down the tube. The next thing I saw was worthy of a Superman movie special effects. Four guys grabbed #4 and threw him out of the mortar pit, perhaps fifteen feet in the air. He was sent to the coast the next day to do – well, something. There are sometimes consequences to policy decisions if one does not understand the environment.

CHAPTER TWO

There was one more event to learn in the Gia Nghia bag of tricks, that was marking for defoliant spray missions which we did three or four times a month. My turn came on 23 November 1968. The spray aircraft were modified C-123, an old medium transport of which there were many doing cargo hauling. The crews were called "Ranch Hands" and their call sign was HADES.

The job of a FAC who had been notified of an intended HADES mission was to fly to the planned start point of the route two hours prior to the scheduled spray mission. He then notified the radio operator of the weather conditions for the route and wind speed and direction – determined by watching tree movement. Assuming that the weather was workable the FAC went and did something else until the formation of C-123 showed up. The C-123 flew in a close echelon formation usually in numbers of seven or nine and made the most awkward radio check-ins I ever heard. It would usually go something like, "Hades Alpha check . . . two, six, four, nine . . ." and so forth. When they were two minutes out the lead navigator would say so and the FAC would mark the beginning of the run with a WP rocket. This was merely a confirmation since the lead navigator was usually very aware of exactly where they were.

The Hades formation had already been descending when they made the two minute call and I marked. They continued their descent to an altitude of about 30 feet before they reached the start point and started spraying, their green camouflage paint job blending slightly into the jungle they slithered across slowly. I continued on the course of the intended spray run flying at 85 knots at the usual 1500 feet. The Hades formation, doing about 130, slowly moved ahead of me. To add some excitement, they always had a fighter escort, usually a pair of F-100, to suppress ground fire. Seven or more slow moving transport aircraft at 30 feet is a target too rich to resist and the bad guys seldom did. They pecked away with small arms fire which started the following sequence. The affected Hades made a ground fire call, an airman on the extended cargo ramp at the back of the affected plane dropped a smoke grenade, I marked the area of the smoke grenade, and the fighters made a couple of passes. That shut up the bad guys until, farther down the run, it would usually happen again.

This whole process was probably a lot of fun for the fighters. They would fly with one on each side of the Hades formation and, given that they were doing at least 400 knots, go into a series of alternating loops, timed so that one fighter was always looking ahead. The bottom of their loops was probably about a hundred feet. It was an odd feeling to have a pair of F-100 climbing and diving in loops on either side of you.

The run was probably 12 miles or so and lead would finally call "spray off" and began a gradual climb away from the run – all C-123 climbs being gradual. The spray would dribble from the airplanes for a while as they climbed away, the fighters went home, and I was left to go do something else – usually more patrolling or stopping by one of the three A teams in the province.

A few days later I flew our O-1 to Nha Trang for periodic maintenance, the trip taking about an hour. On the way back I got a call that there was a TIC (troops-in-contact) situation and, after pushing the power up as much as possible and reaching a speed of 100 knots (gasp!), I arrived at the area of the firefight just as the sun was setting. Don Zlotky, having commandeered one of the Army O-1s, and had already put in some air but he, correctly, figured I needed the practice.

I worked BLADE 01, a flight of two F-100 that had been on alert at Phan Rang. All went well and the NVA broke contact. I was to learn later from the SF team leader that the napalm Blade dropped burst in the high jungle canopy, an impressive picture, but actually only some of it dribbled down the tree trunks. More exciting was arriving at Gia Nghia in the dark. My approach and landing was certainly affected by the radio operator telling me to be careful of the O-1 tail that was sticking up where he had run off the end of the runway. In my mind the tail obstacle got bigger and bigger and my approach got higher and higher. The mortar team illuminated the runway with a flare and I landed safely, although I did use most of our 2000 feet of dirt after my overcompensation. An O-1 had come in from Ban Me Thout to provide an Air Force O-1 but had landed downwind and run off the end of the runway. Thanksgiving was a few days later.

The Army in Vietnam made a big deal out of Thanksgiving dinner and they did a fine job. Everyone from troops in combat situations to everyone else got a hot and good turkey dinner with all the trimmings – if it was at all possible. One of our Army officers had an additional duty of supervising the Vietnamese kitchen staff and he did a really good job for all of us. I had been at Gia Nghia for about three weeks but it felt much longer. It seemed both odd and ordinary to sit on top of a bunker scattered with red dust, after a very large and good dinner, drinking a bottle of Mateus Rose wine (okay, it wasn't great but it was different), smoking my pipe and feeling very content. Everything seemed normal, almost quiet, and my life had settled down. In a few days it would be December and things would change.

The weather on the morning of 4 December 1968 was overcast and wet with dark clouds spotting the horizon and closer. I took off around 0800 to do a weather check on an intended Hades mission on the northwest section of the province near the SF outpost at Bu Prang. The weather was workable and I radioed in my weather report and started heading northeast towards Duc Lap with the intent of checking in with an SF operation named "BANANA DITCH". These operations involved two Americans and a hundred Montagnards that belonged to the "Civilian Irregular Defense Group" (CIDG) at Duc Lap, the standard designation for all Special Forces-affiliated indigenous troops. The operation leader was Sergeant Steele who was originally from Panama. Every operation he ran was called Banana something. This one was Banana Ditch.

I was approaching Highway 13 and noticed that the weather was getting marginal in that part of the province when I got the call on SF common, 35.95 FM. "Any Walt, any Walt, Banana Ditch". Steele's voice sounded a bit urgent.

"Banana Ditch, Walt two-one", I replied.

"Walt two-one, Ditch has been ambushed, need assistance". I could hear small arms fire in the background, sounding like a Western movie shoot'em up. I became very focused.

"Say location". He quickly replied with some rough coordinates. It was about straight ahead and not far away but the weather there didn't look very good.

"Ditch, Walt two-one, will be there in a few minutes, am calling up some fighters". He acknowledged as I flipped the radio selector over to VHF.

"Carbon Outlaw 69, Walt 21 with a TIC (troops-in-contact)". Our radio operator answered immediately and I asked him to put fighters on

CHAPTER TWO

standby but not to launch until I could check the not very good weather. I also asked him to contact the Army Aviation Company in Ban Me Thuot, some 40 miles away, and put some Huey (UH-1 "Iroquois") gunships on standby.

    I had pushed the nose down and increased power to get some speed and to get below the gray fleece of clouds that were getting thicker, darker, and lower as I approached Banana Ditch. In a few minutes I was nearing his location and he confirmed that he could hear my engine noise, giving me some heading corrections. The cloud cover was really bad at about 200 feet overcast with thick veils swooping to the ground in some places. The dark green of the jungle and the tan of the grass in the large "golf course" areas was heavily muted by the woolly cloud cover. This was completely unworkable for fighters so I had Carbon Outlaw cancel them and launch the gunships on what would be a thirty minute trip.

    I found Banana Ditch in the trees and brush along the perimeter of one of the large open pasture-like areas that dotted that part of the province. The terrain was fairly flat but just to the east was one large mountain area we referred to as "VC Mountain". Probably every province in South Vietnam that had any mountains had one named that by the Americans. The North Vietnamese were scattered in the open but were not easy to see given the weather conditions but muzzle flashes helped identify their positions. I had to do something until the Hueys got here with their mini-guns (two per Huey, 80 rounds per second rate of fire per gun, plus a couple of pods of rockets each), but what to do?

    The enemy usually broke contact when a FAC arrived since they well knew that serious trouble would soon follow. These guys didn't break contact and kept maneuvering towards Banana Ditch. Maybe they figured the weather would protect them. I put in one WP rocket to discourage them with an 80 foot diameter 5000 degree explosion but it got too close to Banana Ditch who told me so. I then started making passes at fifty feet, firing my CAR-15 out the left window. At the end of each pass I would pull straight up into the clouds, hammerhead the O-1, and pitch down out of the cloud cover to make another sweep. It seemed to be slowing them down.

In between getting coached by Ditch as to where the bad guys were, I called Carbon Outlaw to have one of the Army guys come and work the gunships since I had to mark for the Hades flight that was due to arrive soon. I fired a total of 120 rounds from my CAR-15 and four rockets before one of our Army compatriots from Gia Nghia arrived. I showed him around the area and then left to go work the spray birds. A few minutes after I left the Hueys arrived and hammered the bad guys with 7.62mm mini-gun fire and rockets. Banana Ditch was able to disengage without casualties.

After working the Hades flight I returned to Gia Nghia where we had a visitor from our squadron, the 21st Tactical Air Support Squadron (TASS). The squadron considered our runway (2000x60 feet of red clay) to be a bit sporty so we didn't get many such visitors. This happened to be the flying safety officer which posed something of a problem for me. There was a rule that you were not to fire your CAR-15 out the window – the enemy had a better chance of hitting you than the opposite and, additionally, some fool had shot his left wing strut off. My problem was that the floor of the aircraft was heavily littered with expended 5.56mm casings. I sat in the airplane hoping the flying safety officer would go somewhere, although there was really nowhere for him to go. The crew chiefs were getting impatient so finally I opened the door and a river of brass shell casings rattled to the red clay ground. Fortunately, the flying safety officer thought it was funny.

CHAPTER TWO

A couple of days later I landed at Duc Lap to talk to Sergeant Steele about one thing that puzzled me. Why, I asked, did the bad guys not disengage when I arrived as they almost always, wisely, did. He smiled a bit and said, "They were mostly women, and women don't quit". It was a little life lesson that I have not forgotten, nor should you.

The weather on 7 December was excellent with sunshine, modest temperatures, and great visibility. I flew a normal observation flight in the morning, landing around ten to turn the airplane over to Don. We talked while the airplane was being serviced and then the crew chiefs and I watched Don take off. It is always odd when something totally unexpected happens and your sensor system – eyes and ears – records the events but your brain has some momentary trouble processing the sensed events. In this case, a genius in the use of a mortar was dropping rounds in front of our O-1 as it accelerated down the runway. The spray of dirt and thump of the explosion finally got translated into a you-gotta-be-shitting-me-we're-getting-mortared-in-the daytime moment. The two crew chiefs and I piled into our jeep, weapons at the ready, and raced through town heading for the compound. The Army crew chiefs were right behind us.

We zipped into the compound where most were already in their bunker positions. We piled out of our Jeeps and headed for our respective bunkers. Some fifteen minutes later Don started working a pair of F-100 (Huns) on the NVA mortar position which was about 300 meters away. The concussion of the Mk 117 750 pound high drag bombs was impressive – it felt like I was briefly floating a couple of inches off the bunker floor. There was an Army Major on the compound who seemed to think fighters carried artillery shells. I could hardly wait to ask him if he still had that thought. Since we were no longer under fire we went our separate ways, I going to the heavily sandbagged command post to find out what was going on.

Taking out the mortar position proved to have been the easy part. A reinforced NVA battalion had moved out of the woods just to the east of the province headquarters and had occupied the small low hills there and had overrun a "model hamlet" (one of the various names used in resettlement operations over the years). Most of the hamlet inhabitants had fled. The NVA were 1500 meters from us and closer than that to the province headquarters. Their opposition was a rotational ARVN battalion that functioned mostly as a palace guard. The ARVN moved to occupy the higher ground and a new US Army advisor, a 1/Lt, the ARVN battalion commander, an ARVN staff officer, and the ARVN jeep driver raced towards the impending engagement. They drove over a command detonated mine – probably about 20 pounds of dynamite – which exploded directly under the jeep. All were killed. Things were getting confusing very quickly.

Army Major Don Chapman, who was the outgoing ARVN battalion advisor, quickly started guiding the ARVN onto a line of low hills slightly above the NVA troops and in a position to defend the town, us, and the province headquarters. Don Zlotky started working the flights of fighters sent our way. The rest of us went to do other things to support the situation. Frank Hilbush, as ALO, stayed in the command post coordinating things while I and the maintenance guys went back to the airfield where a thinned down ARVN company manned their defensive positions. Don landed shortly thereafter and we all did a quick job of rearming and refueling our airplane. I took off immediately to work the next pairs of fighters that would be inbound.

The first thing to do, after establishing radio contact with Don Chapman and Carbon Outlaw, was to get oriented as to who was where. That was more difficult than I had imagined. While the terrain was fairly open, exactly where the friendlies and NVA were was not initially obvious. Chapman was intermittently available since he was running around keeping the ARVN in position. He finally relayed that the province chief wanted the "model hamlet" hit. In addition to the pride factor, it was closest to the province headquarters and did have enemy troops milling around it.

A pair of F-100 checked in and I briefed them on the target and gave them a restricted west-to-east pattern. This went over part of the small town on the west end but that was preferable to the alternatives. Lead made his first pass, dropping two cans of napalm long with no visible results. Two rolled in and pressed his attack a bit too much. His nape was a bit too far south and he hit a tree limb on his pullout. He headed home with his lead flying his wing checking for damage. Two was cussing the whole way – "Been here six fucking months, never seen a fucking target, see one, hit a fucking tree, goddamn sonofabitch . . ." They finally changed UHF frequencies so the strike freq was clear.

I kept bugging Chapman since another flight was due shortly but he was busier than I realized keeping the ARVN focused and engaged. Two F-4 from Cam Ranh Bay checked in and, absent any other targets at the moment, I put them in on what looked like a mortar position to the south of the battle area. It was probably nothing but the airstrike noise had some positive effect. I milled around some more doing visual checks for Chapman and finally landed after a couple of hours. Frank Hilbush took my place and the afternoon wore on.

I was in the command post when the ALO for the 22nd ARVN Division, headquartered in Ban Me Thuot, called Carbon Outlaw on the radio. Lt. Colonel Utsumi started telling the radio operator that he was going to cut off our air support since "we were using too many air strikes". I grabbed the mike before the operator could reply, and ignored the reality that I had made 1/Lt. just ten days before. "This is Walt 21", I started out in an obviously irritated voice, "we're 1500 meters from a reinforced NVA battalion and in contact and you are safe 40 miles away – we'll let you know when we don't need support." I handed the mike back to the operator and left the musty green and tan sandbagged room without waiting for a reply. It made you wonder what this guy was thinking. People focused on promotion would wonder what I was thinking.

Frank Hilbush worked the last set of aircraft, two A-1 from Pleiku well to the north. The A-1 was a large single engine prop driven attack aircraft produced right after World War II. It had a lot of endurance and carried a large amount of ordnance of various types. Frank took full advantage of that and the A-1 whacked away at the NVA for what seemed a very long time. It probably seemed even longer to the NVA. Having done whatever they intended to do, or not, the NVA disappeared into the jungle after the sun went down. It was a tense but quiet night and Frank, Don, and I reviewed our performance, accomplishments, and mistakes. We had worked a total of 9 flights – eighteen sorties – and it had definitely made the difference in the outcome of the day.

There were also some funny stories of the day. Army Captain Gerry Palma was a dynamic character who already had one combat tour with the 101st Airborne. His current task was advising, and encouraging, the local RF/PF ("regional forces/popular forces") – normally a rag-tag bunch of losers at most locations. Gerry's leadership abilities had, however, turned this RF/PF unit into a somewhat capable and aggressive bunch – as we would find out later. During the fighting that day Gerry had perched his RF/PF platoon at the edge of the battle area and was giving them a lecture on what was happening on the ground and in the air and how all that related. He was facing his troops, his back towards the battle area, legs spread, and doing part of his instruction when a 500 pound bomb detonated some 250 meters away. The minimum "safe dis-

CHAPTER TWO

tance" for a Mark 82 was 142 meters and perhaps Gerry thought he was perfectly safe, and perhaps didn't know that "safe distance" referred to troops protected by foxholes or trenches. In any event, a large shard of bomb casing ripped between Gerry's spread legs and imbedded itself in the ground in front of his sitting "students". He turned that into a learning experience and calmly moved his RF/PF unit another hundred or so meters farther away. Gerry was a funny but intense guy and the only person I've ever seen get high on a bottle of Coca-Cola. He transferred to the 1st Cavalry Division a few days after I left Gia Nghia and was killed in action a few weeks later.

The next day I received a couple of important lessons, one more obvious than another. Don Chapman drove me in his jeep the short distance to yesterday's battle area. He was polite but firm as he showed me the first lesson -- the "low" hills he'd been running around most of yesterday. They looked that way on a map and from the air but it was a lot different and more physically challenging on the ground and that was the point. His mildly put reality demonstration was that there were a number of reasons why he, or anyone else in that situation, might not be immediately forthcoming with information. His second lesson of the day was more graphic.

Most of the residents of the "model hamlet" had fled the NVA, but not all. Don led me inside a largish dirt-floored hootch where there were 27 former residents. Each had their hands tied behind their back with commo wire and then shot in the back of the head at close range. The exit wounds in the front of their heads were significant dark red black craters. It was quiet as Don pointed out a few things, all aimed at injecting reality into the Air Force Lieutenant. Flies buzzed and the bodies were a bit ripe. I learned that combat is not some neat and clean thing. I began thinking about the NVA objective yesterday. Perhaps this was it, a lesson that no one could escape them forever.

MEETING STEVE CANYON

Another lesson for the day occurred while I was flying another observation mission, this time looking for yesterday's NVA battalion. Our radio operator called and, making sure that I understood that the question he was about to ask came from Blue Chip and not him. They wanted to know if I realized that I had directed a strike yesterday on a village? My reply was graphically positive. My thoughts were about what appeared to a growing stack of evidence that there was something very odd going on in Saigon.

One night about this time we got the usual mortar attack and the return fire from our compound made a cloud that hovered over the place. Suddenly a twin engine plane sounding something like a C-47 "Gooney Bird" zoomed overhead and a couple of flares were dropped, illuminating the compound with a merciless white light. There seemed to be a universal unspoken agreement among us that the bad guys would give it up for the night since gunships, which is what this had to be, were really dangerous as a weapons system. We all climbed out of our bunkers to see what was happening. I went over to Don Zlotky's location so I could hear any radio transmissions.

It wasn't an AC-47 Gooney Bird after all, but an AC-119 STINGER gunship that had just been introduced to Vietnam and flown by an Ohio Air National Guard unit at Nha Trang at the time. The old Fairchild C-119 was an underpowered transport that few liked. Adding a couple of pod-mounted jets under the wings, like those on the C-123, got rid of the power problem. The AC-119 had four mini-guns (later models had 20mm Vulcan cannon) versus the AC-47's three but it had something much more spectacular that we were about to witness – a Xenon searchlight.

The gunship pilot climbed a bit, turned on the search light, which we had never seen before but Don had heard about, and night turned into day. There almost seemed to be a collective gasp from the three thousand or so people in the town. The gyro-stabilized light rotated and quickly locked on to two bad guys dragging a mortar tube up a cleared sloping area east of the compound. They froze in what I assumed to be terror. The pilot radioed calmly that "this will be a one-gun shot". A second later there was the buzz of a mini-gun and the two NVA became pulp.

Lt Colonel Metcalf was as impressed as the rest of us. "Zlotky", he said, "what kind of a light is that?" "A Xenon light, sir", Don replied. "Well", smiled Metcalf, "we need to get some of those!" Good luck, we thought.

On the 16 December we received a second USAF O-1, on loan so we would have two airplanes. A Special Forces Mobile Strike Force, a MIKE force, was going to do an operation in Quang Duc. They required continuous FAC coverage which meant that in places like ours they lent an airplane. A MIKE force had four US Special Forces guys and 500 indigenous types – Montagnards and Vietnamese in this case. They intended to sweep an abandoned and overgrown tea plantation that sat between the district town of Duc Lap, which also had an A team compound and airstrip, and the nearby Cambodian border. On the other side of that border was a mountain named Nam Lyr. There were rumors, and some evidence, that there were tunnels from Nam Lyr into Vietnam and at least as far as the plantation. I was scheduled for the first flight on 17 December. It would be an interesting day.

The weather was clear with some high cloud when I arrived near the plantation and made radio contact with the MIKE Force. They were maneuvering into the plantation from the south-southeast and the southwest. The plantation, left untended for decades, was probably a couple of miles square and had very dense vegetation growing amongst the old tea trees. Visibility was very poor in that heavy vegetation for the MIKE Force troops and I had difficulty keeping them in sight from directly above. The first contact came less than a half hour after the

MIKE troops entered the southwest side of the plantation. NVA regulars seemed to be popping up everywhere and then disappearing. The friendlies started taking casualties, more troops-in-contact erupted east of the first engagement, and confusion reigned supreme.

The first order of business was to get the wounded out. Checking in with the MIKE force, I quickly called Carbon Outlaw and ordered up some dust-offs – Huey medevac called "dust-off" for battle casualties. Next came the problem of collecting the wounded at a usable pick-up point. Fortunately there were some cleared areas in the center of the plantation. I called MIKE and asked him to relay that I would be making low passes over the clusters of troops I could see and that my heading would be towards the cleared areas. While I was doing this I noticed a group of troops running along the north edge of the plantation. MIKE couldn't clear me to engage because he wasn't sure where everybody was located or what they were doing. As I climbed back to the relatively safe altitude of 1500 feet there was a sudden white smoke burst and flash directly in front of me followed almost instantaneously by a low-pressure whomp feeling in the cockpit. That jolt turned the latching handle on the left window and it popped open. It had to have been an air-bursting RPG. I could see that an inspection panel had been partially blown off on the underside of the right wing.

The troops on the southwest side gradually worked their way eastward through the heavy undergrowth towards the cleared areas. When MIKE and I were sure that group was out of contact for the moment I started adjusting artillery fire from Duc Lap on where I thought the bad guys might be. The dust-offs checked in about the same time that Don Zlotky did. I gave him a quick run-down on where we were, or weren't, and he took over and I headed home. It had been a busy three hours.

CHAPTER TWO

Don worked the situation for another three hours as MIKE gradually consolidated and moved to the east side of the plantation. By the time I arrived MIKE was on the east side of a road in a fairly clear area. The road was crowned giving MIKE about 18 inches of vertical cover in addition to the fairly sparse vegetation. I checked the MIKE commander with my field glasses and saw that he was parked under a tree with thin foliage. They were sporadically engaged with the NVA who were some three hundred meters west. The sky had gone a flat gray with a high overcast when TIDE 01, a pair of F-100, checked in. I briefed them on the situation and called for a south-to-north racetrack while I set up a tight holding pattern just east of the intended pattern. I marked the NVA and cleared Tide lead in hot. They were carrying the standard load of two cans of nape outboard and two 750 pound high drags inboard.

Lead rolled into a shallow dive but he was about 30 degrees off the briefed heading and pointed towards the friendlies. My finger was just pressing the mike switch as he descended through my altitude of 1500 feet, my intent being to have him go through dry – no ordnance release. At that instant three black puffs of smoke spewed from the tail of the single engine F-100. Tide lead immediately called an engine problem and dumped all his ordnance. One high drag bomb hung on its rack for an instant as he pulled up, then released and started in an upward arc towards the friendlies. The rest of the ordnance impacted somewhere around the enemy but I wasn't paying attention. I switched over to the FM frequency for MIKE and told them to stay flat since there was a bomb headed their way. I watched with my field glasses as the MIKE commander and everyone else I could see flattened themselves in anticipation. The bomb detonated about 50 meters from MIKE, the shrapnel ripping down the tree where the commander lay. He was on the radio immediately.

"That was good Walt, but a little fucking close"! Yeah, and embarrassing. Tide flight departed the scene. The NVA troops also seem to have departed.

MIKE moved west across the road and stopped where, by sheer chance, the Mark 117 750 pound high drag had detonated on top of a ventilator shaft that went down into a tunnel system. They put one of the Montagnards on a climbing rope and dropped him down the shaft to see what he could find, not a job I would want. They lowered him down 85 feet to a point where the bomb concussion had caused the ventilator shaft to collapse. Eighty five feet and they had yet to reach the main gallery! This certainly confirmed the existence of a huge tunnel complex that probably did indeed extend the several miles into Cambodia and Nam Lyr Mountain.

I circled overhead while the MIKE commander had a short conference with his US subordinates and the indigenous troop leaders. After a bit he radioed me.

"Walt, we were gonna spend the night here but that doesn't seem like a good idea. Can you cover us while we go back to Duc Lap"? I circled around as they formed up and walked the few miles to Duc Lap, maintaining a loose combat formation. I went back to Gia Nghia after they reached a safe area near Duc Lap.

Six hours of flying that day provided some sobering realizations about enemy strength, tunnel systems, and the limitations of friendly capabilities – at least those available to us. I don't know how many of the MIKE force were wounded or killed but it was not an insignificant number. They did say, the next day, that the NVA troops almost seemed to appear out of the ground in the midst of all the secondary growth in the plantation.

The rest of December was fairly quiet. We had Christmas day off in accordance with an edict that we were not to engage in offensive opera-

CHAPTER TWO

tions. This, of course, gave the NVA a free pass for a day plus. Other than working another spray mission and a couple of sets of F-100 on the resulting ground fire, not much happened. Of course, there was always something on the horizon.

About this time one of the Army O-1 pilots, Dave Vaughn, decided to drive to the Nhon Co SF A team compound to spend some time with one of the NCO there who was going home after a couple of years in Vietnam. Nhon Co was about five miles away and the dirt road was certainly not secure but Dave decided to go anyway. He and the NCO had a few drinks and decided to drive back to Gia Nghia.

Jeeps are not very stable and on the trip back Dave had an accident. He must have had a survival radio with him because Don Zlotky grabbed me and told what had happened and that we and four others were going to go provide security until a Huey medevac arrived from Ban Me Thuot. We drove a few miles towards Nhon Co in two Jeeps and arrived at the scene. The NCO had a compound fracture of his right leg, the femur sticking out through his pants leg. Dave had a broken back. Don and I and the other four took up positions in the tall grass off the side of the road and under the jungle trees while someone else gave basic first aid.

It was an odd feeling being an Air Force pilot lying there with a CAR-15, a round chambered and semi-auto selected, and 15 magazines slung over my shoulder in a bandolier. It was late in the afternoon and the shadows moved through the trees with a remarkable similarity to moving people. I could see how it could be difficult to sort out reality in such situations.

The Huey arrived and slowly flew up the road, under the trees, to where the jeep was lying on its side. It was extremely impressive to me to watch the Huey pilot carefully maneuver so that his rotor tips didn't hit anything. The medic needed a splint for the NCO and asked Don

MEETING STEVE CANYON

and I to give up our CAR-15s since they, with a telescoping stock, made a perfect splint. They loaded Dave and the NCO and then backed out. I don't know how they did it and I was glad I never had to do it! All of us got out of there in a real hurry, Don and I feeling practically naked without our CAR-15s.

In 1981 my wife and I were stationed at Minot, North Dakota. I borrowed a light plane which we flew to a reunion at Fort Walton Beach, Florida. I kept getting into bad weather and didn't feel that I was getting very good weather information from Flight Service on the radio. This problem continued on the way back to Minot and over Illinois I decided to land at the very next airfield and talk to flight service on the phone. We landed at Vandalia, Illinois, which is a very small town. A fat guy with a beard came out and fueled the airplane while I got on the phone to flight service. We decided to spend the night and while we were waiting for a car from a motel the fat guy and I started talking.

He asked what I flew and I told him that now it was the B-52H but that after pilot training I'd been an O-1 FAC in Vietnam. "Where were you", he asked? I told him it was a place no one had ever heard of, Gia Nghia. His eyes narrowed," when were you at Gia Nghia" he asked? When I told him he smiled and said," I'm Dave Vaughn".

January was not much of an event horizon for me since it included a total of four TIC airstrikes, three spray missions, three sets of helicopter gunships doing SF team infils and exfils, and the usual number of SKYSPOT observations which strengthened one's skepticism if nothing else. We did get the usual number of mortar attacks but even that was barely enough to fend off the boredom. One evening we were sitting on benches on the concrete pad outside the "officer's club" as sundown neared. A few were idly watching two dogs hump – a true sign of boredom – when there was a distant sound of small arms fire.

CHAPTER TWO

The firing increased and seemed to be moving closer. Someone went to the command post and learned that Gerry Palma's well trained RF/PF unit, unlike most of their peers elsewhere, had actually attacked an NVA unit that was enroute to conduct its periodic target practice on us.

We finished our drinks and ambled towards our bunkers picking up weapons and flak jackets along the way and waited for things to start. The two bunkers on the other side of the compound that had .50 cal machine guns lined up their guns on the likely location of the mortar tubes the NVA would be bringing. We didn't have to wait long. At the first tube flash of the NVA mortar the two .50 cal and four or five .30 cal M-60 opened up on the mortar position. Perhaps another mortar round got fired and that was it. No bodies or equipment were ever recovered in such circumstances but that evening's show was abruptly cancelled due to a fully prepared audience. Things went back to being quiet.

Walking to breakfast one morning I watched briefly as two enlisted Army types moved themselves into a bunker on a permanent basis, having had enough of the persistent mortar attacks. This was a bit of an over-reaction I thought but as I watched them I was horrified to see the current residents depart the bunker.

Recall that during mortar attacks someone was the first sliding down into the darkness of the bunker and no lights were ever used in that blackness. The current residents of the bunker I was looking at were not fond of humans so they were headed elsewhere. A number of thoughts raced through my mind as I watched two largish cobras slither away. Of course, creatures that did like humans moved into that bunker – rats, of which we had plenty.

One sunny afternoon after flying I was sitting in the sunshine reading a recent edition of National Geographic magazine. There was an article and pictures on Oregon including some great shots of the Portland Rose

MEETING STEVE CANYON

Festival Queen. Ignoring the fact that I hadn't seen a round-eyed woman for a few months, she was an absolutely fantastic blonde. I slipped the issue into my map bag, intending to show it to the SF guys at Duc Lap the next day. It was another warm and sunny day when I landed at Duc Lap and was driven in a jeep to where they were perched on two connected hilltops. We went over the local situation for a while and then I pulled out the magazine and showed the pictures of the Rose Queen to the senior NCO team chief. He looked at her a long time, looked at me very sincerely, and said, "sir, I bet she shits strawberry ice cream". That line has stayed with me since.

A day or so later I checked in with the Duc Lap radio operator on 35.95. He gave me some coordinates and asked me to check the place out. A quick look at a map told me it was triple canopy jungle which meant I had to have some clue as to what I was looking for in 200 feet plus of swirling green. I asked him what I was looking for and he said he couldn't tell me. Sigh. I explained reality and he reluctantly informed me that it was a two and a half ton truck (deuce and a half) and they didn't want the bad guys to steal it. How in hell, I asked, did the truck get where it was? Oh, it was dropped by a helicopter from two thousand feet. Having seen a truck dropped from fifty feet I told him not to worry. However, I could imagine a group of NVA sitting around a cooking fire talking when a big truck came hurtling through the jungle canopy and smashed to pieces next to them. That would have been an interesting follow-on conversation to hear.

Other than attending the 0800 Province headquarters meeting a couple of times a week, I had no contact with the locals other than passing them on the way to the airfield. Don Zlotky was a different case. He had a passion, perhaps an obsession, for taking pictures. One that he took from the airfield got me in a bit of trouble with Frank Hilbush.

CHAPTER TWO

It was a great shot looking down from the airfield to the town below. If you looked closely you could see about one third of the wing of our O-1 jutting past the roof of a house at an altitude of perhaps five feet. Since Don was taking the picture, clearly I was flying the airplane. Frank was not amused. Don drove all over the local area taking pictures of about everything.

One evening when we entered the officer's bar there was a dirty entwined box-like package with some wires sticking out of it. When we asked what it was one of the Army officers addressed himself to Don saying, essentially, that Don's picture trips were more dangerous than he thought. The cruddy package was a command-detonated mine that Don had driven over that day. Fortunately for him the Vietnamese who was supposed to do the detonating had stepped away to relieve himself and had been neutralized in one way of another. Don's picture-taking travels declined considerably.

One of the Vietnamese officers I saw occasionally at the Province meetings was Major Anh, a man of many skills I was to learn. One night during a mortar attack, while in our bunkers, someone thought they saw troop movements below us on our side of the compound. The bunker next to us popped a hand flare and yes there were troops. The adjoining bunker opened fire with their M-60 machine gun, but we did not and that was fortunate. The ARVN had started a sweep around our compound in an attempt to snare the shooters. Nice idea but they didn't tell anyone. We were all lucky that no one got hit by the machine gun fire. Major Anh, however, had a message to deliver.

During the next mortar attack our bunker took one round on each rear corner and one directly in front of our central firing port. There was significant blast effect and dirt swirling around as we got shaken like dice in a cup. The next morning we looked at the mortar tail fins that remained

37

and found that they were all 60mm, while the NVA used 82mm. Major Anh, the mortar master, was sending a message. It was my turn at the Province meeting that morning and I sat next to Anh. He leaned over with a slight smile on his face and said, "watch who you shoot at". Okay. If he knew I was in that bunker why didn't he know the bunker next door did the shooting? We will never know.

The trigger-happy tendencies of the next door bunker were demonstrated once more during what I will call the great sock mystery. You could have your clothes "washed" by the Montagnard maids, or for a modest price you could have stuff done by a Vietnamese family who lived in a hootch downslope from our bunker. While they did an okay job, almost all our socks gradually disappeared. The Vietnamese man, who did speak some English, insisted that he had no idea where our socks had gone. One day I was in picking up my laundry and an Army Captain from the trigger-happy bunker was yelling at the Vietnamese about socks and how he would shoot up their hootch. During attacks the Vietnamese bolted down a hole into their own bunker so they would be safe no matter who was doing what. During the next attack the bunker next door sprayed the laundry hootch. In the morning I went down to pick up laundry and there were hundreds of socks available for the taking, the Vietnamese man chattering and smiling and bobbing up and down. I took some socks and went back to the compound wondering what motivated the great sock theft compulsion. Is this what defeated the French, all their socks getting stolen?

Our mail got delivered two or three times a week by an Australian Air Force Caribou light transport with the call sign of WALLABY. For some reason we didn't get any mail for three weeks and most were a bit grumpy about it. I was flying around one overcast gray day with nothing going on when I heard Wallaby call Carbon Outlaw. "Outlaw six-nine (you'll

CHAPTER TWO

have to supply the Australian accent), Wallaby zero six, we're ten miles out with 700 pounds of mile (mail) for you Yanks!" I headed back to Gia Nghia since getting some mail was more important than the boredom I was experiencing. After landing I drove to the compound and stood in the long line of people eagerly awaiting their mail. There were lots of grins and laughter as people thought about all the good things they would hear from home, and I was no exception. Then I got my mail, a bank statement. Well, it was funny in a way.

Sometime in the latter part of January there was an ARC LIGHT (B-52) mission that dumped their load (324 750 pound M-117 slicks) in a 1x2 kilometer box in the eastern part of the province. A MIKE force came in behind the Arc Light to assess any damage and engage any enemy troops that might be there. We got our usual extra O-1 so I was droning around over them waiting for something to happen and to act as a radio relay between the MIKE force and their SF command element in Ban Me Thuot. I did get a call from Ban Me Thuot in which they asked me to relay a Vietnamese name. They spelled it and I wrote it on the right window in grease pencil (all FAC carried a grease pencil) and confirmed the spelling. I then relayed the name to the MIKE force. They made no contact during their sweep but they did have one man killed. Someone had discovered an agent and that problem was solved.

Our division ALO, Lt Colonel Utsumi, appeared at Gia Nghia one morning and talked for a while. I was then supposed to fly him back to Ban Me Thuot in the MIKE force O-1 where they would pick it up. The airplane seemed to have some power problems and I felt like I had to fight it up towards 1500 feet. I finally quit fighting at 1400 feet and we rumbled towards Ban Me Thuot. Utsumi was not very happy with me being 100 feet lower than the Air Force wanted but it was hardly a big deal. I made a normal landing that quickly turned into not so normal.

MEETING STEVE CANYON

Landing a bit long on the 3000 foot strip and bouncing quite a bit was somewhat embarrassing. I then added power for a go-around – as I would at Gia Nghia – and found that the engine wouldn't accelerate the O-1 past about 52 knots, about three knots above a stall. Now I was at about 50 feet, a line of trees ahead, couldn't climb, and not enough runway left to make a landing. About this time the Army tower operator asked if he could be of assistance. I didn't have time to formulate the reply that I wanted to transmit. In my peripheral vision I could see Utsumi tightening his harness. Then I saw it ahead, a hole through the trees, undoubtedly made by some larger aircraft. I pushed the nose down to get a little airspeed, flew through the hole, got enough altitude to make a pattern, and landed again.

It was a good landing and all was well until I neared the parking area for the Air Force Birddogs. When I put on the brakes to stop, the right brake hydraulic line ruptured and sprayed hydraulic fluid on the hot brake. The fluid immediately caught fire. Fortunately, a crew chief was there with a fire extinguisher and took care of that problem in a few seconds. I got out of the O-1 followed by Utsumi. He glared at me, shook his head, and walked away. I never saw him again.

There was a guy in civilian clothes who lived off the compound but would occasionally stop by our officer's club and have a drink or two. When I asked him one night what he did he said that he was part of the "Province Reconnaissance Unit" or PRU. He didn't elaborate but did say that he was a former SF NCO and would be mighty bored when he returned to his civilian job as a welder in a Seattle shipyard. One day I saw him, at a distance, hiking into the jungle with a rucksack and a rifle, but not an ordinary rifle compared to military issue. It looked like a pretty good sized hunting rifle with a large scope on it. I later learned that the PRU was really the operational end of OPERATION PHOENIX,

CHAPTER TWO

a CIA managed joint program intended to assassinate or capture VC personnel. While it made perfect sense in theory – certainly better than having a hundred US troops shoot up a village – it had a major weakness in having to rely on Vietnamese intelligence sources. Too often in such situations, "bad guys" may simply be someone who has pissed off someone in the tribal or semi-tribal hierarchy.

The farther away one got from the large bases the better the food got, generally speaking. Ours was certainly good and well worth the "closed mess" fees I paid. Occasionally, however, we would run out of things and sometimes for a considerable period. We had not had fresh vegetables for weeks and it was surprising how you develop a craving for something like that. One day a Huey pilot kicked off a crate of green onions. Three of us sat down outside and ate every onion. They tasted terrific! Ten pounds or so of green onions does induce a certain amount of stomach acidity!

Other than pissing off the division ALO, eating too many onions, and getting mortared some more it was a pretty boring January. I asked if I could take some leave, which was approved, so I arranged to go to Hong Kong in early February.

CHAPTER THREE

Hong Kong was preceded by a couple of days and nights with one of the F-4 squadrons at Cam Ranh Bay. At that time the Air Force was assigning pilots right out of pilot training to the back seat of the F-4, a practice which caused a great deal of bitterness by placing a junior pilot in a demeaning (in their mind) navigator position. I had originally been selected for a back-seat slot coming out of pilot training but I found an arithmetic error in Training Command's computation of my class standing so I got to select the O-1 FAC job. My brief time at Cam Ranh convinced me I had made the right decision since the front-seaters and back-seaters seemed to be in constant conflict.

Cam Ranh was a very large base perched on the Gulf of Tonkin, essentially immune from hostile action, and would have made a great beach resort. It was a nice couple of days of eating, drinking, and a little beach time with the F-4 guys and their nurse friends. I gawked a bit at the nurses. My invitation to the F-4 pilots to come visit Gia Nghia was met with looks of horror and I found they were prohibited from such visits. They seemed to regard me as recklessly brave and perhaps very foolish for living where I did and doing what I did. They, I thought, ought to see line infantry up close. In any event, I processed through the R&R center and got on a Pan American 707 headed to Hong Kong.

MEETING STEVE CANYON

I sat in an aisle seat next to an older looking Air Force Major who, it turned out, was an A-1 pilot so we had something to talk about. His accent sounded a bit odd, sort of like Brooklyn but not quite. Charleston, South Carolina he said, an original accent. He advised me to stay at the Park Hotel since that is where all the flight attendants stayed. I also talked to some Red Cross "donut dollies" (intended to set up entertainment and so forth for the troops (no smirking!). I asked one of them what they did and her reply was that they visited Army facilities and set up things like ping pong tournaments and so forth. I guess my face was blank when I commented that I'd never heard of that. There was a slight smile on her face when she remarked that in their experience the Air Force knew how to entertain themselves. I returned her smile and some thoughts ran through my head but she had just become engaged and her companions were clearly her protectors.

The two hour flight was routine but the approach to Hong Kong's Kai Tak airport was not. It was extremely weird to be sitting in an airline seat, watching, as the 707 arced around a radio tower on a tall hill as it reversed course and then flew down between tall buildings before emerging in a clear area just prior to touchdown. Impressive in another way was the R&R in-processing, run by the Army in Hong Kong. It was a very slow, tedious, and boring and it took almost an hour to escape.

The Major, who had been to Hong Kong several times, suggested that we go out to dinner. We went to a steak house sort of place in a Chinese city with at least 5000 restaurants, but it was actually pretty good. I had my first escargot experience and liked them enough to have three dozen at 90 cents a dozen. My room at the Park Hotel was large and comfortable, and quiet. I slept tight that night – no sirens, no bunker, and no artillery.

The restaurant in the Park Hotel had high ceilings and arches that suggested perhaps original construction in the nineteen twenties or so

CHAPTER THREE

but the whole place has been renovated several times since I was there. Near the end of a very good breakfast I watched a lesson in basic counter-insurgency. Toast came on little racks – this being a British colony. A Brit, a few tables away in the sparsely populated dining room, loudly clapped his hands and almost shouted while glaring at the waiter, "Boy, this toast is cold!" The waiter barely hid his utter contempt while he went to get fresh toast. The Brit didn't seem to realize that imperial rule was over and that if you want cooperation you don't be obnoxious.

Another counter-insurgency lesson also occurred in a restaurant. This time it was Jimmy's Kitchen which had been in Shanghai before the Communists took over, and is now in both Shanghai and Hong Kong. They had both Western and Chinese food and it was obviously an upscale place. I ordered carpetbag steak and it was terrific. A couple at a nearby table finished dinner, paid their bill, and then stood up, the wife berating the waiter in a loud voice with a Long Island accent. She poked her finger at the waiter's chest as she announced to all that " . . . this isn't real Chinese food, we got real Chinese food on Long Island, and this . . ." You could spot the GI's in the place, they were the ones thinking about crawling under their tables. I don't know about the others but I left a 100% tip.

The weather was nice if slightly chilly and I did all the obligatory things which, in Hong Kong, meant getting clothes, shoes, and jewelry made, shopping for domestic stuff like tableware – and sending it all to my mother's house in California. One of the Pan Am flight attendants and I had lunch on the chilly deck of the Tai Pak floating restaurant that was almost a scene out of the film "The Sand Pebbles".

One odd experience happened one sunny afternoon while I was crossing from Hong Kong to Kowloon on the storied Star ferry. I was standing outside, leaning against a deck rail, when an attractive but demure young woman, at least partly Chinese who was standing next to

45

me, asked if I was an American. When I said yes she replied that she was going to college in America soon and would like to ask me some questions. While it sounds like a prostitute pickup she looked completely out of character for that – although I'd been fooled before. After the ferry docked we walked a brief distance to an upscale hotel and had tea. She told me that her father was a British civil servant and her mother was Chinese. Her whole conversation hinged on what was either great acting or true deep naiveté. When I asked where she was going to college she said the University of California at Berkeley. I pondered a few seconds, wondering if she knew what Cal Berkeley was like in 1969 and if I should say anything to give her a reality check. I didn't and we parted ways after our tea. I have occasionally wondered, assuming she was real, I think she was, and how her life progressed.

Mostly, however, I thought about where I was in Vietnam and the usefulness of what we were doing, or not doing, in Quang Duc. It wasn't that I was having visions of grand strategy, but more a sense that I was engaged in a reactive futility and that there was little chance for me, or the people around me, to affect the course of the glacier of events that was moving towards us. Part of that thinking was spurred by the 7th Air Force directed pre-plans that Don and I worked at the direction of someone who thought they were doing something productive, but weren't and they didn't know the difference and, it appeared, didn't much care as long as that square got filled and they looked good . It might have helped the situation if 7th Air Force had directed a FAC to check out an area instead of relying solely on their problematic "intelligence analysis". Another part of my uneasiness was the sense that we were delivering pinpricks to a flowing mass of enemy that we couldn't quite define but it was certainly large. If nothing else popped up I'd finish my year at Gia Nghia. If something else surfaced, I'd probably do that something.

CHAPTER THREE

Since I was on leave there was no seat reserved for me on the R&R flight back to Vietnam, but there was always some kind of traffic. After a week plus of having a good time I caught a hop on the DC-4 assigned to the US Ambassador to Vietnam. The plane, stuffed with toys to be handed out at the soon to arrive Tet New Year holiday, was a comfortable ride to Saigon. We landed at Ton Son Nhut airfield late in the afternoon and I immediately called the ALCE (Airlift Command Element) to see if there were any flights going north to Nha Trang. The guy who answered the phone was a pilot training classmate, Curt Fischer, who was doing a brief tour at the ALCE instead of flying a C-130. After we got over our mutual surprise he told me that there were no flights north until the morning and that I could sleep in an extra bed in the old hotel where he was staying. That sounded good to me.

We had a couple of drinks and dinner and then headed to the off-base hotel where he lived. Having been carrying a sidearm and, most of the time, a CAR-15 for the last four months, I felt extremely uncomfortable being unarmed and said so. Curt, being unarmed, felt no particular anxiety. My hyper-awareness really began pulsing when we checked in with the "guard" outside the hotel. It was a teenage Vietnamese kid who did not appear to have the means, or probably the motivation, to stop any bad guys. When we got up to Curt's fairly large room on the third or fourth floor I went into a defensive posture. The first thing I did was open the large bathroom window looking for an escape route. A drainpipe ran vertically next to the window and was held in place by large brackets typical of older French construction. Good! The brackets were large enough to work as a rudimentary ladder.

Curt was staring at me like I was crazy when I pulled the mattress off the bed next to the door and dragged it over towards the bathroom. Then I moved the bed so that it blocked the door from being opened.

MEETING STEVE CANYON

Okay, good enough. I had a good night's sleep. Thirty years later, at a reunion, Curt told me he still thought I was nuts. Perhaps I was, but a live nut.

I got to Nha Trang the next day but had to wait until the next morning for a ride back to Gia Nghia. Once again fate smiled on me.

The 21st TASS operations officer, Major George Tynan, had set up a room next to the Officer's Club for squadron visitors like me. While it didn't sound fancy, having two double bunk beds, it did have air conditioning and that was a very big deal since only Colonels had air-conditioning at Nha Trang. After dinner at the O'Club I was sitting at the bar having another drink when a guy from my FAC school class sat down next to me. We were the first wave of pilot training graduates to go directly to a FAC assignment. Tom Gresch was a COVEY FAC flying black-painted O-2 over the Ho Chi Minh trail at night working with Special Forces teams in an operation named PRAIRIE FIRE. It was demanding work and he was doing a good job. He was never in Nha Trang except for a SF meeting he had to attend so this was pure luck, or destiny. I described where I was and what I did and expressed some of the thoughts I had reflected on in Hong Kong. He took another sip of his drink, looked around, and then focused on me.

"Tell your ops officer that you're interested in Steve Canyon", he said. "What's that", I asked. He shook his head slightly. "That's all I can say."

Major Tynan shared a room at the 21st TASS with three other officers. He had piercing blue eyes and a no-nonsense demeanor when it was necessary. I asked if I could talk to him and he held out his hand towards a chair next to his desk. After a short bit of small talk he asked what he could do for me.

"I'm interested in Steve Canyon", was my reply. He paled slightly and said that might not be such a good idea. I persisted a bit and he finally

CHAPTER THREE

nodded his head and said he would put me on a list but it would take some time, and to not mention this to anyone. I thanked him and left.

That was the 12th of February and when I arrived at Gia Nghia later that day, after being gone 12 days, it seemed as if little had changed. I slipped back into our normal routine, working a spray mission the next day. About that time one of the C-123 transport planes that we relied on broke down on our runway. The crew was evacuated since spending the night at Fort Apache was considered out of the question. The next day a C-123 maintenance crew and replacement aircrew arrived, fixed the broken airplane, and all departed. We all thought it a bit odd that the NVA had not taken the opportunity to mortar a sitting duck lightly defended by a somewhat sleepy ARVN company who, after all, couldn't do anything to prevent a mortar or RPG attack on that duck.

Our unspoken thoughts were seized by one of the Army Captains whose part-time job (they all seemed to have part-time jobs) was being the Psychological Warfare (PYSWAR) officer. He came up with an air-droppable pamphlet that called the NVA, essentially, a bunch of light-weight cowardly wimps for not attacking that C-123. He, a big grin on his face, asked Don and I what we thought. We told him he was nuts and not to piss off the bad guys since we already had enough problems. Soon thereafter an O-2B, a Psywar airplane, landed at Gia Nghia – a sporty proposition for him – and took on the leaflets which he dropped somewhere.

This event sort of disappeared off our radar but we did notice that we didn't get mortared for some three weeks. On February 23rd, however, some of us had an interesting and revealing experience.

One of the few district towns in the province was on a river that defined the border between Quang Duc Province and Dak Lak Province to the northeast whose capital was the city of Ban Me Thuot. Farming was not considered practical around those towns so the United States provided the rice that kept the population going. One of the Army guys noticed that the rice ration going to this town, Duc Xuyen (duke schwin), would feed about 500 more people than actually lived there. So, the ration was reduced accordingly. It turned out that there actually were an additional 500 people eating that rice furnished by the United States – a 500 man NVA battalion. The battalion, pissed off about the lack of rice, took over the town and we had a TIC situation.

Once again we had two airplanes and Don was there first. I took over when he departed and the situation was very confusing for a number of reasons. The first was that we didn't realize that we were dealing with a NVA battalion although I'm sure the small number of ARVN troops understood that. There were troops milling around the town but I didn't know whose they were. A Huey dust-off had landed slightly south to take on ARVN wounded. He could also see the troops milling around and asked me if they were friendlies. I told him to standby. I got the District Chief on the FM radio and he assured me that they were friendlies. I passed that on to the Huey who proceeded to take-off straight ahead, to the north, over the "friendlies". He immediately took numerous hits, shattering his windscreen and having a couple of rounds go between his legs. He got the Huey back around to his take-off position with some difficulty and was very irritated with me. I didn't blame him. Well, now we knew who and where the bad guys were.

I worked a pair of F-100, SABRE 05, in a west-to-east racetrack in an attempt to attack the NVA even if it meant blowing down part of the town. Unbelievably, on lead's first pass the two cans of napalm he dropped not only missed the NVA, they missed the whole town, tumbled across the river, and impacted on the far shore. That was embarrassingly bad. Sabre 05 didn't do much better with the ordnance they had left but

CHAPTER THREE

the friendlies finally got in a defensive position they could hold and the day was over.

I didn't know what Steve Canyon meant but if it got me out of this sort of situation, I was ready. Consider what was going on here. The District Chief, in addition to lying to me about who were the friendlies, was feeding an NVA battalion, supposedly his avowed enemies. The Province Chief was clearly involved. Rather unlikely that this was the only example of this in South Vietnam. There was no way this was going to turn out well. The response to all this from our side was to increase the rice ration to its previous levels. While we didn't sit down and have a general discussion about this, I think there was a general sense of unease.

When I was assigned to the Pentagon in late 1973 in the intelligence systems division, I visited an intelligence library in the vault next to mine. In the library there were copies of all the MACV (Military Assistance Command Vietnam, the overall headquarters) reports on every province in Vietnam. Quang Duc, of which we controlled perhaps 20 square miles out of 2500, was listed as "secure" in every report. When an organizational culture requires that reporting be "positive" in order for the person reporting to advance in the structure, there will be a serious or fatal consequence to the organization's mission somewhere down the line. There is reality out there and trying to tap-dance past it does not work. There have been more recent examples of this approach, all of them having negative consequences.

A few days later I worked TIDE 21, two F-100, on a 7th Air Force pre-plan. A good FAC, or a good photo-interpreter, can tell if a footpath is being used to haul supplies. The weight of supplies, and the number of people involved, gradually adds depth and width to a footpath making it a trail. I arrived at the designated target location, described as a supply route, to find a Montagnard footpath intersection that had probably

51

been there for twenty years, or a hundred. The photo-interpreter who thought this was a target and the approval chain was, in the kindest of terms, not very experienced . We dutifully blew down some trees and the month ended on a sour note.

The efforts of the Advisory Team's part-time PSYWAR officer a few weeks before finally paid big dividends, but perhaps not what he might have desired. Early in March we experienced a mortar and RPG attack far beyond anything that had occurred while I had been there. A small crowd had formed outside the door to our room where they sheltered waiting for some slack in the incoming before, one by one, making for their bunkers. A near constant stream of mortar rounds caused dull booms and orange flashes seemingly everywhere. Hand flares popped from our bunkers as troops looked for a possible ground assault. RPG seemed to zip past from nearly every direction as our small crowd thinned down to just two of us. As the other guy and I waited for a slack cycle to the mortar fire I experienced an overwhelming commanding thought – get your gas mask. My rational mind quickly replied that was silly. Get your gas mask came back the command.

I turned away from the other guy and took two steps back to the door to our room. Pushing open the door, I reached in and lifted the gas mask container off the nail where it hung. I turned around and as I did so slung the mask container over my left shoulder. The other guy was gone and I had just barely started to move back to a waiting position when an RPG air-burst right where I would have been had I not experienced, and obeyed, that command that came from somewhere. I jumped into the concrete drainage ditch in front of me and crawled a short distance. There was plenty of orange and white light from explosions and flares as I crawled out of the ditch and under a jeep and headed for my bunker. My progress was suddenly stopped by something that jerked on my left shoulder. In a couple of seconds I realized that the gas mask container had caught on something on the underside of the jeep. Cursing, I slipped the mask container off, flipped it up into the front right seat of the jeep, and resumed my crawl towards the bunker. In front of me, about where I would have been if I hadn't got hung up under the jeep, an 82mm mortar round detonated. Well, two for the night I thought.

I quickly exited the cover of the jeep and was making good time towards the bunker when the strap on my new Seiko watch popped open. There I was, on my hands and knees, resetting my watch band when one of my bunker mates yelled at me from the entrance hole. "Get in here you dumb sonofabitch"!!! It always helps to have someone around to bring you back to reality. I scampered on my hands and knees the 15 feet to the bunker.

I had previously experienced a bit of what I would call "mental messaging", but nothing on this level. In the first instance a person I knew was "sending me a message". This case was entirely different and would be the first of many such experiences. While the scientific community may blow off such experiences, I and many others can relate to extraordinary events that occurred after, it seemed, we breached an emotional or mental wall. While it may not be scientifically definable, it is real.

The part-time PSYWAR officer got another chore to accomplish. We had been running short of various types of food and Lt Colonel Metcalf was getting annoyed. He sent the Captain to Cam Ranh Bay to collect an unspecified but large amount of various kinds of food. Metcalf correctly pointed out that they had everything you could think of at Cam Ranh. Three days later, an Army Chinook heavy lift helicopter arrived with a 6000 pound sling load of food. That was terrific but that was a whole lot of food for 75 guys and we had limited refrigeration and freezer capacity. What to do? Well, obviously, eat a lot. We had what amounted to a three day food orgy mostly centered on beef and fresh lobster, Vietnamese lobster being very good. At breakfast on the third morning I let out a fake groan, "What – lobster omelets again!"

I was sitting in our always-dark room one afternoon while writing a letter by the dim light when I heard the distinctive noise of a Chinook helicopter. It seemed that the big helicopter was headed towards the compound and not the airfield. I put down my pen, wondering what the hell was going on, when the Chinook arrived over us churning up a tornado of red dust that filled every room on the compound. In less than a minute the rain of red dust subsided enough for me to open the door to see what was happening. Glancing down towards the latrine I saw a guy who must have been in the shower when the storm landed. He looked like some kind of mud-man movie horror creature with his eyes sticking out from a layer of running red mud.

Lt Colonel Metcalfe had decided that we needed four machine gun towers to help defend the compound. The towers had been dutifully built by our local Army Engineer who somehow got the job done despite the lack of appropriate equipment. Then the good Lt. Colonel Metcalfe had reasoned that if the bad guys got inside the compound they would be able to shoot up through the bottom of the towers therefore negating the utility of the tower machine guns (you are correct, this makes no sense). So, the idea was to sling-load in 6000 pounds of armor plate to put on each tower. The Chinook had gone blind in the red dust, the armor started swinging, and the pilot dumped the load. Gia Nghia seemed to have a lot of miracles since no one was hurt – but yes, pissed off. The Air Force retired to the airfield when the next such event was scheduled.

The weather was good in March with few overcast days. I worked one spray mission and three pre-plans in four straight days. The pre-plans were the usual tree-busters but the last one, four VNAF (Vietnamese Air

CHAPTER THREE

Force) A-37 with the call sign of JACKPOT, was particularly interesting. The four VNAF pilots had come out of years in the A-1 to fly the light attack A-37, a converted trainer, and were exceptionally experienced, each with thousands of combat hours. Lead spoke some broken English while the other three spoke none. The A-37 were carrying 8 250 pound bombs each. I briefed the flight and marked, telling lead to hit my smoke since there was really nothing there to hit and we all knew it. Lead promptly dropped one bomb directly on the spot where my rocket had landed. I gave a correction to lead to pass on to two but there was no time. Two, three, and four each put one bomb directly on lead's first bomb crater. I gave lead some new direction and we repeated this again, and again, and again. In the end four aircraft had dropped 32 bombs and left 8 bomb craters smoking in the jungle. I would have loved to have had those guys around with a troops in contact target – but only if we could all speak English.

The month wore on with two more spray missions, three pre-plans, and one Huey gunship operation covering a hot exfil. The last few days of March involved working multiple flights in two successive days on troops-in-contact situations. One involved a heavily contested exfil of friendlies from a hot LZ. In one standard TIC, good guys versus bad guys were facing each other, I was talking via FM to the engaged SF unit commander while we waited for the fighters to arrive. He commented that he thought my job was pretty dangerous, flying around in a slow airplane where everyone could see you. While he talked I get hear the sound of heavy gunfire all around him and I wondered if he was crazy or just being sarcastic. While we were talking some more I heard a definite thump and he made a strange noise, and I thought the worst had happened. He was back on the radio in a few seconds and I asked him what happened. "Some sonofabitch just shot the stock off my rifle!" I couldn't

MEETING STEVE CANYON

resist. "Yeah, it's pretty dangerous up here." I lit another cigarette as the fighters checked in and we started hammering the bad guys.

Then on 28 March 1969 my world changed forever. Our radio operator received a message from the squadron that I would be picked up in the morning and taken for an interview with the commander of the 504 TASG, based at Bien Hoa to the south in III Corps. I brushed off questions with the answer that I didn't really know why, which was mostly true.

About mid-morning an O-1 arrived, flown by a Lt. Colonel I had never seen before. There was nothing sinister about this since the squadron seemed to have a lot of spare Lt. Colonels doing whatever. I climbed into the back seat and we flew the hour or so to Bien Hoa, making a stop at Bao Loc about halfway there for the Lt. Colonel to talk to Ed Lauffer, one of O-1 FAC there whom I had met before. Ed's living conditions were miserable from a safety standpoint. The Gia Nghia compound was on a hill, the one at Bao Loc was in a terrain bowl that allowed the bad guys to shoot down on their target. Ed and another guy shared a good-sized room but they had created a maze of wall lockers to confuse a night-time enemy who would someday arrive. I would see Ed again.

The interview with the 504th commander, Andy Chapman, was a bit of a joke. He had been there only a few days and had obviously been coached on what to say. I did learn that I would be going to Laos, I would be TDY (temporary duty) from my current squadron (not normal), and that this was a portion of what was termed Air Force Project 404 and that Steve Canyon was the cover name for the FAC portion of that project whose call sign was Raven. We would operate in civilian clothes in unmarked airplanes. He did say that I was to resist any offers of money, perhaps $25000, from drug dealers who might want me to haul opium in an O-1. I thought it would have to be a pretty desperate drug dealer

CHAPTER THREE

to haul opium in an O-1. I didn't do anything obvious like spitting on the floor so it appeared that I had passed the interview.

An obvious question at this point is the why of all this secrecy in the myriad of situations in Southeast Asia. In the aftermath of the French defeat in 1954 her former colonies became the nations of North Vietnam, South Vietnam, Cambodia, and Laos. The political situation in Laos was complex and unstable, partially due to the competing influences of North Vietnam, the Soviet Union, the United States, China, and to a lesser extent, others. A neutrality treaty, the Geneva Accords, was signed by all parties in the summer of 1962. The United States honored the treaty, as did most of the others, but North Vietnam, supported by the Chinese and Soviets, did not. This led to a more than gradual escalation of involvement by all the major players. The southern portion of Laos became a critical supply route (the "Ho Chi Minh trail") for the North Vietnamese supply of the Viet Cong and NVA regulars in South Vietnam. Laos was also important because it provided a potential shield for Thailand which, in the early sixties, was ill-prepared to engage regular North Vietnamese forces should Laos become an open pathway to Thailand.

While the United States escalated its efforts in Laos by a variety of means, it was deemed important that effort should not become too obvious to the outside world because of the treaty. This was the reason for the secrecy surrounding US operations, including Steve Canyon. If this sounds somewhat silly, it was as will later be described. Obviously, the violators of the treaty; the US, USSR, China, North Vietnam, Thailand, and the various Lao factions were all well aware of what all the other parties were doing, as were other signatories of the treaty, but no one complained because that is the way things were. First Lieutenant Polifka was expected to play the same game.

MEETING STEVE CANYON

The Lt. Colonel flew me back to Gia Nghia where a message was waiting for him. He told me I had 15 minutes to pack – and to make sure to take some civilian clothes, and we would be going to Nha Trang for the night and I would be flown to Saigon in the morning. I threw my stuff in a largish A-3 parachute bag and an issue B-4 bag and we were on our way. I had exactly six months in Vietnam, a total of 440 hours in the O-1, and had worked a total of 72 sorties of fighters – 36 airstrikes.

In the morning I was flown to Saigon in an O-2 by Ken Sellers who had spent years in Vietnam so he wouldn't be sent back to SAC to fly bombers. He taxied up to base ops and the nearby courier service, Scatback ops. He shut down and I pulled my baggage out of the airplane, said goodbye, and walked towards Scatback. The courier service was located in good-sized office type building attached to a large aircraft hanger. I was about to walk through the looking glass.

CHAPTER FOUR

Two other guys were waiting outside Scatback and seemed to know that I would be the third and last in our group. We introduced ourselves and talked for a few minutes before going inside. One was Dan Davis from III Corps with about two months in-country. The other was Dan Berry from I Corps with something like three months in-country. It was pretty obvious that the other FAC squadrons were not following the rules of the game which demanded six months experience. There could be a number of reasons for this ranging from significant personality frictions to getting rid of accidents-about-to-happen.

We went inside and proceeded to a wood paneled air-conditioned office where a somewhat smug looking Lt. Colonel sat behind a fairly large wooden desk. He was reading the Asia edition of the Wall Street Journal, his reading glasses perched at the end of his nose. We presented our orders and stepped back as he glanced at them, and us, with annoyance and palpable disdain. "The C-118 (DC-6) that was supposed to take you to Bangkok is down for maintenance. Come back in three days." He dismissed our presence by going back to reading the paper. We went outside to consider our options and wondering why a trip to Bangkok, not that we would object. None of us wanted to spend the night at Ton Son Nhut, all having done that once which was enough. Berry said he

MEETING STEVE CANYON

would call the 504th TASG and I decided to go see a pilot training classmate who was stationed at Tan Son Nhut.

When I got back a half hour later Dan Berry said he had gotten through to Bien Hoa and they said they would take care of it. We decided to slither back into the Lt. Colonel's posh surroundings and see what happened next. He gave us a look of disgust and was about to say something when his phone rang. We almost started laughing when he popped to attention and started spluttering answers to the caller. "Yes, General . . . yes . . . they're standing right here", he glowered at us, " . . . yes sir, we have a T-39 going to Udorn right now . . . but General, there are three full Colonels on that airplane . . . yes sir, yes sir." He put the phone down, picked up a microphone that was on his desk, and directed a T-39 to stop taxiing. He gave us another hate look for the few seconds it took for an enlisted guy to come in and help us with our bags and drive us the short distance to the T-39 (a North American Sabreliner executive jet) which was stopped on the ramp.

Three Colonels got off the T-39, a bit dazed to see three First Lieutenants taking their place. An enlisted guy on the T-39 helped us load our bags, pausing for a moment to stare at the flash suppressor of my CAR-15 which was sticking out of my A-3 bag. We got strapped in, the door got closed, and we started taxiing. The crew chief gave us each a cup of coffee and seemed pretty deferential. All things considered, it certainly wasn't a normal day for him. We all looked at each other, smiled, talked quietly, and agreed that whatever this program was it was pretty damn good so far!

We arrived at Udorn RTAFB in northeast Thailand after about an hour and a half. After deplaning in front of base ops one of us called a phone number we had been given for transportation. The base was spread out in front of us and was busy with its two F-4 fighter squadrons and

CHAPTER FOUR

one RF-4 reconnaissance squadron. It was a clear hot day with the sun reflecting off the seemingly endless concrete taxiways and ramp space speckled with protective revetments. Then there was another part of the base from which came our transport.

We piled our bags in the back of a six-pack truck and the driver made what amounted to a U-turn and we drove towards a taxiway ramp area towards some nearby two story buildings and hangers on the left and a largish two story more modern building on the right behind its own set of fences and razor wire. A Thai guard waved us through and we drove to near the end of the ramp area where we got out. This was Detachment 1 of the 56th Special Operations Wing. The Wing itself was located at Nakhon Phanom RTAFB which was southeast on the Mekong River. The primary purpose of Det 1 was training pilots for the Royal Lao Air Force (RLAF), which explained the dozens of T-28D aircraft on the ramp. It was also where our records were kept along with any uniform items we might have.

We were taken in hand by Airman Spence whom we came to refer to as ex-PFC Wintergreen, a notable character in the book Catch-22. Spence, a jovial and perceptive individual, took our paperwork and told us we had to change into whatever civilian clothes we had. After doing that we stored any uniforms we had in a CONEX shipping container. In my case that was a set of SF Tiger stripes and camouflage jungle fatigues, which I never saw again. Spence then drove us to the headquarters of the 432nd Tactical Reconnaissance Wing, the imposing regular Air Force presence. As we drove down the ramp he pointed out the hangers which housed Air America maintenance operations. The fenced-in building on the other side of the ramp was, he explained, the Joint Liaison Detachment or JLD. What, we asked, was that? The CIA, he said with a slight smile.

MEETING STEVE CANYON

The purpose of going to the Wing headquarters was to get the paperwork completed and pictures taken for our escape and evasion information. Each of us provided questions, and answers, which could be asked via emergency radio to verify our identity before a rescue helicopter was committed to a rescue attempt. We were also issued, as we had been in Vietnam, 9 x 20 inch silk sheets with the US flag on it and a description of us, in many languages, as US citizens. These were called "blood chits" since they offered a reward for our safe return. We also had our picture taken, the escort officer telling the intelligence section not to ask us any questions. Not quite James Bond, but the feeling was there.

After that Spence drove us back for our bags, less our survival vests and CAR-15, and then to the billeting office so we could get a room for the night. After that, we were on our own after acknowledging the instructions to be at base ops in the morning for a ride to Vientiane in the Air Attaché's C-47 (Douglas DC-3) transport. We checked out the officer's club, had a couple of beers, and headed to downtown Udorn where billeting had leased a very plain hotel type structure. On all future visits Ravens stayed in very decent downtown hotels.

Udorn was a mass of mostly two story buildings that bustled with people that were friendly and smiling. The people contrasted significantly from the Vietnamese who, after 25 years of war, were a surly bunch. I was to learn that the nearly universal Thai smile could also mask anger but the overall impression was of a societal sunny disposition. Udorn's streets were paved, vehicles of all sorts driving on the left, and the town was crossed with occasional canals (klong) that held stagnant water, some trash, and plenty of breeding insects. Dinner that night was at the Siri Udorn Hotel. It was a modest place, as most places in Udorn were, but the food was very good. We all had Kobe beef filets packed

CHAPTER FOUR

with blue cheese for the equivalent of $2.50. Of course, it was marinated water buffalo but it still tasted great.

We were in base ops in plenty of time to catch the Air Attaché (AIRA) Gooney Bird ride. The attaché, Colonel Tyrell, introduced himself in a somewhat perfunctory manner and we all boarded for the brief flight to Vientiane, the "Administrative Capitol" of Laos (as opposed to the Royal Capitol in Luang Prabang much farther north). Tyrell remained a distant character whom I only saw twice more in the nine months I would be in Laos.

The three of us were met at Wattay airport in Vientiane by Raven One – Mel Hart who was a Lt Colonel. Mel shepherded us through the check-in process at the AIRA office where we chose our Raven numbers for Long Tieng, our destination to the north, one of five Raven locations. I became Raven 45. We then went to the US Embassy where we received State Department identification cards and then to a local tailor where we had flight suits made in a color of our choice. I was appalled that Dan Davis ordered a dull blue color as if this were a fashion show. The best single color to be wearing if you were evading in the jungle is black, which is what I ordered. Mel then drove us around the town showing us the sights.

Vientiane was interesting in many respects but the one overwhelming impression that I remember was the sense that it was still an old French colonial capitol town. Life seemed to move slowly, most of the buildings were from another age and showing it a bit, the shops and marketplace had a wide ethnic variety of merchants. The large number of old Citroen cars driving around certainly added to the colonial impression. It would not have been too surprising to see Humphrey Bogart driving past. That impression was certainly reinforced that night when Mel took us by a couple of celebrated institutions for a closer look. One of them was "The White Rose", a brothel run by a French Madame who had been a camp follower to a Foreign Legionnaire. The Madame, and others like her, had operated in Vietnam but were forced out by the Diem regime who declared there was no prostitution in South Vietnam -- an interesting, if deliberately delusional, concept on the regime's part.

The bottom floor of the dimly lit White Rose was filled with low tables and thinly upholstered chairs. Madame stood at the bar, controlling the liquor and, more importantly, access to the brothel cubicles on the second floor. A 45 RPM Victrola record player sat on the bar and played one record, apparently the only one Madame owned. Little Richard's "I got a gal named Boney-Maroney" played over and over, with occasional breaks. The interesting part is that there were a number of flat spots where the continuous playing had worn the record flat. When the record player got to those parts it just hissed. One other interesting feature of the downstairs part of the White Rose was the couple of "waitresses" that worked the tables. They were actually prostitutes and marketed their wares by wearing only panties. For the equivalent of a dollar (200 Kip in Lao currency) they would do a brief version of a lap dance intended to interest the recipient in further action upstairs. Mel paid our waitress her fee and pointed out the intended target. This led to one of the more foolish displays of human behavior that I can recall.

Two French couples had entered and were sitting at a table for four located against a wall where they were having a drink. It was an odd place to come for a drink with your wife, but who knows? Mel had pointed our waitress at the French guy sitting with his back to Madame. The French guy's wife was seated against the wall, making him an easier target. The waitress went over and did her stuff, including rubbing her breasts around the guy's head. The guy waved the waitress away. The wife was clearly annoyed. Mel gave the waitress some more money and

CHAPTER FOUR

she repeated her act, perhaps with a bit more intensity. This time around the French guy got up, grabbed the waitress by the hand, marched up to the Madame, paid his fee and went upstairs to do his thing. The guy's wife was really furious and got into an animated discussion with the other couple which, it being in French, I couldn't follow. Finally, the wife stood up, pulled the car keys from her purse and waved them at the other couple before storming out the door. One would suspect that things would be extremely tense in that household.

The next morning we picked up our new flight suits and were driven back to Wattay to the Air America terminal building where Mel arranged for us to be on the next transport to Long Tieng, otherwise known as LS (Lima Site) – 20 A (alternate) and often referred to as just "alternate". We had been repeatedly briefed about the secrecy of the Steve Canyon/Raven program, particularly by the AIRA office. It didn't take a lot of reasoning to see how this could not actually be much of a "secret" but we were certainly not going to get talkative. While we were waiting a young American woman started talking to us. She was, she said, waiting for an Air America flight to Bangkok to see a dentist. The fact that she was traveling on Air America certainly indicated some connection to the US government. Finally she asked, "what do you guys do"? We sort of looked at the walls and floor and hemmed and hawed. She smiled again, "oh, you must be the new Ravens". Some secret!

Our flight was called and we walked across the ramp with our bags and got in the back of a silver C-123 for our flight north. We had left Vietnam 48 hours before and it seemed like a week. We were in a different world.

CHAPTER FIVE

The typically noisy ride in the C-123 flight to Long Tieng took about 35 or 40 minutes. We couldn't see much while sitting in the cargo compartment but on final approach I looked out and saw mountainsides flashing past just before we crunched down on an asphalt runway. We taxied briefly, swung around, and the cargo ramp lowered so we could get off easily before the cargo pallets were removed. It was a bright sunshiny day and, given the elevation of 3200 feet, a bit cooler than what was normal for us. A ridgeline swept up to the northeast with a lower one to the southwest. The patched asphalt runway ran southeast to northwest with a large spire of limestone karst at the northwest end. It was obvious that you took off to the southeast down that long runway that sloped increasingly downhill. We were on a sloping asphalt ramp that was crowded with a variety of helicopters and C-123 and Caribou transports, soldiers, cargo, and trucks all busy and all in motion. It would impressive in most places but after the isolation of Gia Nghia it was particularly impressive. A large white jeep pulled up and the driver motioned to us to get in.

He introduced himself as Larry the radio operator as he helped us toss our gear into the jeep. He drove around the northwest end of the runway, slowed, and pointed out aircraft wreckage at the base of the

MEETING STEVE CANYON

karst where someone had tried a go-around that hadn't worked out very well. It was a few hundred yards to our destination, a somewhat rambling one story weathered teak house on stilts on the side of a modestly sloping hill. Larry led us to our room on the back side of the house where there were three bunk beds, a chest of drawers, and a couple of wall lockers. We picked our bunks, I took the top one since I was taller, and we followed Larry for a quick house tour.

On the side of the house towards the road was a good sized living room with a fireplace. The living room doubled as a dining room for the 12 people that lived there – plus the three houseboys who kept things cleaned up. On the downslope side of the living room was a screened-in porch and bar. In the kitchen was the cook, Manual Espinoza, known as Espi, working away at his food inventory. Espi, an Air Force Staff Sergeant, made life much easier for everyone. There were three or four bedrooms on that side of the house and three on our side plus a room for Espi and the radio room. I never did understand exactly where the houseboys slept. The toilets, showers, and 85 gallons of hot water were in a separate building near the kitchen. Next door, up the slope, was the much larger CIA house. Downslope was a good-sized concrete CIA communications building which also had a room for small meetings. The view from our house included the runway and General Vang Pao's two story cinderblock house on the northern side of a good sized compound situated southeast of the runway. The valley had something like 25,000 Hmong (then called Meo) living in it, a small but growing number of Thai support and combat personnel, and the handful of Americans from CIA, Air America, Continental Air Services International (CASI, part of Continental Airlines), and the Ravens and their support personnel.

By the time we got unpacked and organized the Ravens were coming home to roost. This included Paul Merrick, soon to go home; Fred Platt,

CHAPTER FIVE

who was taking the one month leave that came with a six month tour extension, and Jerry Hare, both of whom would soon transfer north to Luang Prabang (LS 54): Dick Shubert, a Major and the senior Raven, who would be leaving soon; and Bob Passman who had recently arrived. We all met in the bar area, had a few drinks, and exchanged introductions and experiences while Espi got dinner ready.

We were advised to eat lightly since we would be going to General Vang Pao's house for dinner, a customary evening ritual, and to be introduced to VP, as he was called. We were also advised to stick to the sticky rice and vegetables since the meat dishes were of unknown origin and probably a bit exotic. By the time the maintenance guys had finished their work and had a drink or two the houseboys had set up the dinner table and we all sat down and we new guys introduced ourselves to the ground crew.

By seven o'clock we were seated in the large social area of Vang Pao's house. There were probably 35 or 40 people at this evening ritual intended for social interaction between Vang Pao and the hierarchy of the various clans, village chiefs negotiating favors, and, of course, with the farang (foreigners). Vang Pao was in his early forties then, a short man with a commanding presence who had unified the Hmong clans in a common cause – the first time this had happened in centuries. His dark eyes exhibited a very high level of situational awareness, intelligence, and resolve. He had been in combat of one sort or another for over 20 years and had been wounded at least a dozen times. He had been recruited, and his standing enhanced, by the CIA in the early sixties since it was clear that he was the linchpin that could hold this part of Laos as the events that were sure to follow as the Geneva Accords unfolded.

The Hmong had been engaged in a protracted guerilla operation against the much more conventional NVA for years. The support for this operation, and those in the rest of Laos, came from a Presidential Finding in the early sixties that involved the CIA as the lead organization but also included USAID, the State Department, the local American Embassy and their assigned military attaches, and the Department of Defense. Numerous Hmong base camps, each with at least a rudimentary dirt airstrip, were scattered through Northern Laos and were known as "Lima Sites". Each was supplied by Air America and Continental Air Services. The Hmong conducted fairly successful irregular warfare from those sites with some obvious strategic limitations. They made the NVA (and the Pathet Lao Communists) pay a high price for their operations, but there was little likelihood of "victory" in a conventional sense or a blocking of the NVA from Laos. Among the tactics used by the Hmong was to engage an NVA unit, holding it in place briefly while a Raven worked air strikes on the NVA. Over time, however, the Hmong lost most of the important sites north of Ban Ban Valley and the overall situation was getting a bit grim.

Vang Pao was well aware of reality and he was very conscious of the costs to their population in general and young men in particular. The draft age was 15 and there were many 12 and 13 year olds engaged in combat. The North Vietnamese had virtually limitless manpower. The Hmong had no replacements.

After a ritual shot or two of CIA-supplied White Horse Scotch we gathered at VP's large table which seated probably 15, about half being Americans that night. Dick Shubert, introduced us to the CIA guys and VP. I noticed that the experienced Americans were wadding up some sticky rice in a hand and dipping it slightly in shallow saucers that held some sort of clear liquid with a few seeds in it. I followed suit but my foolish mind told me that more was better so I really got a lot of sauce on the rice and popped it into my mouth. Drinking gasoline would

CHAPTER FIVE

probably have been more comfortable! My eyes watered but I got it down alright, burning all the way. I tried to avoid obvious choking. The atmosphere seemed to be charged with a certain level of tenseness and focus that the three of us had not been experiencing. There was going to be a lot to learn.

Part of that learning process continued when we left VP's house and headed back up the hill to the next item on the agenda – a meeting in the CIA comm center where we would briefly review priorities for tomorrow and scan available intelligence. The interior of the comm center held a number of well - lit desks in a large center area where the communicators plied their trade. Around that center area were some enclosed office cubicles with lockable doors. On the left side was a small conference room. During my time I went to the comm center most nights, but some Ravens did not. That was very unfortunate because it was there that the people running the operation you were supporting made available to you a range of intelligence products that gave you excellent insight into who was doing what next and where. This was a far cry from Vietnam where we received very little information/intelligence from outside our narrow world.

The weather was pretty bad for a couple of days so we occupied our time with making a master navigation chart with each of the 48 something 1:50,000 charts marked on it; plus folding, marking, and storing the 1:50 in a map bag. Sounds boring but you need to do that if you are going to cover 8000 square miles and be able to rapidly tell precisely where you are. We also spent time learning how very different the availability and use of airpower was for us versus what we had experienced in South Vietnam. We also learned a couple of other things about our new home. Our water came out of a local stream. The houseboys boiled our drinking water for half an hour. That water was then put in a cistern in the kitchen. When you actuated the tap on the cistern the water flowed through a ceramic filter intended to remove whatever was left after the half hour boil. When I held a glass of water up to the light there was always a few things floating around but our doc said it was just dead stuff. Unh huh! Another lesson was our TDY pay. It had been at the "non-availability" (no government housing available) rate of $16 per day. Some finance guy decided that we indeed did live in government housing (whose government?) and cut that to $8 a day. Fred Platt retaliated by creating a $2 per day "BOQ fee". In the end the Air Force saved about $100 a day. We worked up to $2 million a day in ordnance.

The considerably larger CIA house was next door upslope from us. We did not go in their house except on very rare occasions but we did spend a little time on the back side of the house with their "pets". These consisted of a family of papa, mama, and two youngish offspring Himalayan Black Bears. The adults were around five feet tall and probably weighed about 250 pounds. The male, Floyd, had developed a fondness for beer and wine and had something of a drinking problem. The bears had a good-sized cave in the karst and steel bars had been built outward from the cave entrance so the bears could also have outside time. There was a terrace on top of the cave/cage complex where you could sit and talk and drink on nice evenings. An enclosed bar would be built there in a couple of months. The new bar would come complete with an opening through the floor to the bear cage so that Floyd could receive fresh cans of beer.

In our new environment the Ambassador and CIA negotiated a percentage of all available tactical air power for our use in supporting CIA-run operations. That airpower flowed to us steadily during the day (or night, but we normally didn't work nights) and was funneled through an airborne command and control (ABCCC) C-130 to whatever Raven

CHAPTER FIVE

had the most urgent requirements – decided by the airborne Ravens bartering on FM. We decided what targets to strike, and with what resources, based on our knowledge and CIA priorities. This meant that we had a very fast reaction time to evolving tactical situations or high value targets. This also meant that the scads of Colonels and Generals in Saigon, who had very little sense of the battlefield or regional experience, had little to no influence on how or where we used the airpower they generated. This did not make them happy, which we were to later learn the hard way.

After spending a couple of afternoons of playing bridge to fill my spare time the weather improved and I was given an orientation of much of the working area by Fred Platt. I climbed in the back seat of an O-1F and the lessons started. The CIA, called "the customer" or CAS (Consolidated American Sources) had dictated that Ravens had priority in the traffic pattern. This meant that when a Raven made a taxi or takeoff call the Air America and Continental traffic held unless they had an emergency. The runway was about 4200 feet long and its slight downward slope became more pronounced the farther you went down the runway. The low end of the runway would be good for a high speed abort but many of the aircraft there didn't have the climb capability to get over the rising terrain. After you got airborne a slight right turn was a good idea since there was an imposing piece of karst hillside almost runway centerline about half a mile from the downhill (southeast) end. Since there were no runway lights, night landings would be sporty as I was to discover. During Fred's tour I followed along as he pointed out the spectacular mountainous geography, Lima Site locations, friendly troop dispositions, and recent battle activity. Near the end of his instruction for the day he worked six F-105 and two A-1 on a variety of targets in the Xieng Khoung area. The trip home to Long Tieng included him pointing out a couple of stream beds that could be used in most circumstances if the weather was too bad for a normal approach.

A number of things were clear to me beyond the difficulty of the terrain and the large operating area we would cover. My main observation was that random attack patterns by the fighters should be the norm in most situations. A random pattern essentially consisted of the attack aircraft flying a circle around the target, usually seven to nine thousand feet above the target (for jets, "fast movers"), and then rolling in sequentially so that attacks were constantly coming from different directions. These were necessary because of the heavy ground fire and, to some extent, the terrain. The down side of this for the FAC was that he was in the neighborhood of the fighter's dive recovery altitude, greatly increasing the potential for mid-air collisions. Near misses were normal and avoiding them demanded constant awareness. Then there was the weather which could change quickly and make things more dangerous. Total focus and situational awareness were critical not only for effectiveness, but for survival.

What were the differences in ground fire from where I had been and where I was now? The ground fire scope and intensity varied in South Vietnam. Certainly in the north in places like A Shau Valley, there was plenty of 12.7 mm (.50 caliber), 14.5mm ZPU, and some heavier stuff. In Quang Duc Province we got periodic small arms fire that was ineffective if you were at 1500 feet – where the Air Force wanted you to be for that very reason. Where I was now was a whole different story and it was not a place to bring the engine to idle, a la Vietnam, before rolling to mark a target. That signal to the enemy would get you a face full of lead in Laos.

In addition to heavy small arms fire, you could expect 12.7 mm in many places. Add to that ZPU and a great deal of 37mm. The 37mm, a World War II era AAA gun, traversed relatively slowly and was therefore

CHAPTER FIVE

usually protected by two or more 12.7 mm. One quickly became used to the supersonic snap as near-misses zipped past and eventually, with lots of exposure and practice, it became possible to see some rounds going past. All of these weapons heavier than small arms could shred an O-1 or, in the case of 37mm, blow it to pieces with a one round hit. For this reason, in this environment, consistent flying behavior was a very bad idea. While the O-1 was slow, constant random slight variations in heading and altitude made it tougher for the bad guys to get you. Another tactic that I adopted was to fly above 2500 feet while en route to my intended work area. This was about the maximum effective altitude for 12.7 mm while ZPU fire was effective to about 3500 feet. Others preferred to fly lower and that was fine also, as long as we were collectively unpredictable.

There is a phenomenon experienced by many who have repeated high intensity exposure to combat. While it is not "scientifically provable", it does exist. Things appear to slow down substantially in these conditions. Yes, you can see bullets and they appear to be moving fairly slowly. Yes, dropped bombs move at what seems a slow enough rate that you know where they are going to impact. Yes, you do seem to sense unfolding events at a slow enough pace so that you can react and avoid developing unfavorable situations, sometimes. That doesn't mean you become invincible, you simply become hyper-aware of events as they develop and you seem, to some extent, to be forewarned.

On April 7th I finished my checkout with Fred Platt and in the course of the day, flying twice, worked 18 sorties of F-105 under a high overcast. While we didn't take a lot of ground fire this was not an easy job when one considers that 18 fighter sorties was one quarter of the air I worked in six months in Vietnam. A couple of days later I checked myself out in the U-17 which was the Military Assistance Program (MAP) version of the

MEETING STEVE CANYON

Cessna 185. Many of the early Air Commando types really liked the U-17 for a number of reasons. While it did have seven hours of fuel, it picked up speed very quickly in a dive and, being a side-by-side airplane, it was difficult to see outside compared to the O-1. This particular day involved hauling two Hmong around on what amounted to a sight-seeing trip to LS-184 which was very north in Military Region II, our operating area. One of the Hmong was a senior type in VP's entourage and looked remarkably like an American Plains Indian and, therefore, was called "the Indian". I felt like he was there to evaluate me and it was a bit annoying. The other Hmong fell in the category of "backseater".

Ambassador Sullivan, who just departed Laos, had directed that all Ravens would fly with a local "backseater" (later called a Robin) who would communicate with the locals at Lima Sites, to ensure that the Raven understood the wishes of the locals, and act to prevent collateral damage if possible. That may have been useful early on but times had changed in a couple of years. The local guy on the radio at a Lima Site spoke very understandable English thanks to a CIA training program. The backseaters tended to have limited to no English capabilities and it seemed to me and others that their job was acquired through political connections as a means of escaping ground combat. I, for the most part, stopped carrying backseaters after being there a few weeks. The first reason was that I detected what seemed to tribal/clan retribution via airpower. This is not uncommon in these types of situations. The second reason, and perhaps more important, was that many Asians are not good air travelers, particularly if the airplane is doing a lot of maneuvering while taking ground fire. Having been the victim of projectile vomiting that gushed onto my neck and back too many times, I stopped putting myself in harm's way, so to speak. That decision was probably a relief to our houseboys who did the washing.

CHAPTER FIVE

Before we started that first U-17 ride a couple of the Air America Filipino ground crew took my picture in front of the plane. They gave me prints of the few pictures they took. All pictures taken at Long Tieng were supposed to be processed by CIA to assure that no pictures were inadvertently taken of their case officers. About a year later when I was stationed at Hurlburt Field in the Florida Panhandle I noticed that the prints they gave me were on commercial, not government paper. I called Joe Potter, who later in my tour was the "AOC" ("air officer commanding" of the local T-28D unit and a former Air America pilot who was also at Hurlburt) and asked him about the paper. He told me that the Filipino maintenance guys made extra money by taking the pictures and passing them on to North Vietnamese intelligence contacts in Vientiane who, in turn, passed them along to the KGB and Chinese intelligence service. That gives one room for pause.

I got another "inspection" ride when the chief of the backseaters, Vang Chou, showed up at the house one morning and announced that he would be flying with me to the Xieng Khoung area. Vang Chou had taken an AK round through his right armpit while flying in an O-1 back seat. The round had cut the nerves depriving him of any control of that involuntarily clenched hand. There wasn't anything going on around Xieng Khoung and he spent a lot of time showing me various sights. I headed back to Long Tieng as my fuel got low. The weather had deteriorated significantly and I was in a canyon following a stream that had been pointed out by Fred Platt, periodically flying blindly through clouds. It was a bit disconcerting to come out of a cloud and find a canyon wall off one wing tip or the other.

About that time there was a burst of Hmong on the VHF and Vang Chou told me that Vang Pao wanted me back at Xieng Khoung right now! I half turned in my seat and pointed to the wing root mounted fuel float gauges and explained that we were too low on fuel. Vang Chou then proceeded to pull his CIA issue Browning Hi-power out of his holster with his left hand. I turned forward and told him on intercom that he could shoot if he wanted but he wouldn't be able to fly the airplane back to Long Tieng in this weather (or any weather, for that matter). He holstered the Browning.

I asked a lot of questions about Vang Chou that evening and was better prepared to deal with him should that be necessary. The most useful point was that the hit in his armpit happened while he was at low altitude. Sure enough, he showed up the next day insisting that there was big trouble at a LS off the Southwest corner of the PDJ not that far from Long Tieng. When we got there it was clear that there was nothing going on and that this was another Vang Chou game. The trees in the area around the site were not too close together. I spent about 20 minutes zigging around between the trees and below their tops before Vang Chou allowed as how he wanted to go home. He was not a happy camper after we landed but I never had any more trouble from him.

On the tenth of April a new Raven, John Bach, arrived. Having been there 10 days I fell into the category of "old head" and was selected to check Bach out as Fred Platt had done with me. Bach had spent six months in IV Corps in the delta of South Vietnam where it is mostly flat and he was not familiar with the perils of mountain flying. I flew with him a couple of times and felt he would do okay but was uneasy about two things. He flew too close to the tops of ridges and blew off my warnings about potential mountain-wave effect. The look on his face said he wasn't interested in hearing about advice concerning ground fire, jinking, and not being predictable.

After getting a brief check-out in the T-28D, Dick Shubert came back to 20A for a few more nights before departing. I got two flights in the

CHAPTER FIVE

back of the T-28 and found it to be a lot of fun. It seemed like a rocket compared to the O-1 although the T-28 only cruised at about 140 with an ordnance load. One of the guns jammed during the second flight and the actions of some of the ground crew confirmed some suspicions. Two or so of our ground crew of six were short-term fill-ins and seemed a little slow on the uptake. One of them, nicknamed "Greek", was staring down the barrel of a .50 caliber machine gun while it was being cycled to see why it jammed. It didn't seem to occur to him that he might get his head blown off. A few days later one of the other short-term guys said to me that we were working them too hard and that maybe they would do something to the planes to slow down the pace of our flying. I reported this to Dick Shubert's replacement, Don Service. Don was a pleasant but no-nonsense F-105 pilot who certainly appreciated the implications of that. The short-term guys were gone the next day.

Every day involved flying a couple of sorties of about three plus hours each and working numerous strikes, weather permitting, in difficult terrain and often significant ground fire. The day started shortly after dawn with the turbine howl of Air America and Continental Pilatus Porters, a single engine Swiss-built STOL cargo aircraft capable of handling the worst of the numerous Lima Sites. That was followed by the rumbling engine start and departure and arrival of C-123 and Caribou transports. There was no sleeping in unless the weather was completely unworkable which was, by our standards, unusual. Having said that, our weather limitations were pretty rigid, compared to Air America and Continental, since we had to get fast-movers down through the weather and work in visibility conditions that permitted them to see the target. Air America and Continental pilots and crews were true professionals who not only flew in extremely marginal weather, but operated from airstrips that were nightmares to most pilots and often made 30 or so takeoffs and landings per day in such circumstances.

Another chore I acquired was writing up recommendations for decorations. This started after Platt, who had done this previously, moved on. The administrative officer at AIRA sent a bundle of Fred's hand-written paperwork and asked for somebody to clean up the mess. The Air Force regulation on this was included. There was less work than it looked like because most of Fred's "recommendations" were simply not possible. A company grade pilot is not going to get a Legion of Merit, period. I typed everything up to make the admin guys happy and also included recommendations for Distinguished Flying Crosses for the five Ravens who had participated in the "Long Tieng Escadrille" episode the month before. On that occasion the five Ravens and a backseater had flown three O-1 across the Plain of Jars in bad weather, unworkable for fighters, at low altitude to where an NVA battalion was overwhelming some Hmong forces. The Ravens -- using AK-47, grenade launchers, and 2.75 inch flechette rockets – broke up the NVA attack. The Hmong then took the offensive and routed the enemy. The AIRA office had threatened to have them face courts-martial for, well, something. Perhaps, I reasoned, cooler heads had prevailed. They eventually did and each guy got a DFC.

The 20th of April was another one of those days. There were six Ravens at 20A – myself, Berry, Davis, Passman, Service, and Bach. We staggered our takeoffs so that there would always be at least two Ravens airborne to handle the continuing flow of airpower. Don Service was working the northern part of the PDJ in the late morning while I was in Ban Ban valley and Bach was working the Xieng Khoung area where a protracted battle in March still flared from time to time. Don and I received a radio call from CRICKET, the ABCCC C-130 that Raven 44, John Bach, had been shot down and killed and that friendlies required our assistance. Don and I,

CHAPTER FIVE

about ten miles apart, started towards the Xieng Khoung area as fast as our respective O-1 would go.

I headed towards the karst that defined the east end of the remains of the town, running at full power and in a slight descent. Don beat me to the town by about a minute and I heard him checking in with a case officer as I started rounding the karst at an altitude of perhaps 20 feet. I glanced right towards the karst and in a stunning instant saw a 37 mm gun, in another instant it fired and my mind recorded the recoil ripple on the vegetation, and in another instant the 37 mm shell passed between the propeller and the windscreen of my O-1 – a distance of perhaps five feet. Considering that I was traveling about 170 feet per second you can figure the odds. I immediately turned left and descended to almost ground level while flying down slightly sloping terrain away from the gun. They fired twice more, barely missing my retreating figure.

I flew down a road and then climbed so that I was in a holding pattern directly over the large hill just south of the town so I could see what was happening and, if needed, replace Don Service who was beginning the process of taking out the three active 37 mm and six or eight 12.7 mm guns on the main road running out of the town. There is usually no good reason to take out AAA guns just for the sake of taking them out – a very dangerous process with an absurd risk/reward ratio. However, in this case, General Vang Pao and case officer Burr Smith along with a contingent of troops were no more than 500 meters to the south and upslope from Route 4. We had to get Burr and VP out of there and that meant the AAA had to be taken out. Don was already in contact with the flight of F-105 that had been inbound to Bach, briefing them on the situation including the friendly positions.

The F-105 (with a high accident rate it was referred to as the "Thud", the sound it made when it hit the ground) rained Mark 82 on the gun

MEETING STEVE CANYON

positions, but not their CBU (cluster bomb unit, see glossary) 24 because VP was too close. The guns, particularly the 12.7, were firing so much that I lost sight of Don several times as his whole airplane was obscured by tracers. The fire slackened a bit as the bombs detonated, but it didn't end. Using my field glasses I could see some of the crews were killed or wounded but replacements immediately ran into position, throwing bodies out of the gun pits and continuing to fire. The Thud flight lead was enraged and rolled into a steep dive and began a long strafe run with his 20 mm Vulcan Gatling gun. As aircraft speed increases in a dive the nose tends to rise. The flight lead was "bunting", running the elevator trim enough to counter that. He also fired for about four or five uninterrupted seconds, undoubtedly burning out the Vulcan as it spewed out 100 rounds per second. I watched the rounds concentrate in the gun pit – perhaps a 10 by 10 foot area – pulverizing both the gun and its crew.

Don continued to work strike after strike until all the guns were destroyed and their crews killed time after time, and Air America could extract VP and Burr. Don and I, both low on fuel, flew back to Long Tieng for some lunch before flying again that afternoon.

Late that afternoon I spotted a stationary PT-76 tank on the PDJ. This was an unusual sight and I expected this to be a flak trap, which was not all that unusual. NEWARK, a flight of three F-105, was headed home with 20mm remaining and Cricket diverted them to me. 20 mm strafe would shred a PT-76 so this could work. In briefing Newark I said this was probably a flak trap so there would be no more than one pass each, if that. As I rolled in to mark a 37 mm round passed close enough behind my rudder that the rudder pedals jumped. I saw the 37 mm muzzle flash to the west, marked, told Newark about the 37 mm, and cleared him for one strafe pass. He hosed the PT-76 and, it having thin armor, undoubtedly destroyed it. The 37 mm crew had, unwisely, positioned themselves

CHAPTER FIVE

just east of a low ridgeline which restricted their field of fire to the west. Ten minutes later I worked HATCHET, another Thud flight, on a west to east run which turned the gun into scrap metal. All in all, it had been a shitty day and another reminder that this was a very tough environment.

Our house was a comfortable place, if a bit crowded. Espi seemed to have an overwhelming desire for pork but, other than that, the food was adequate and, most importantly, we didn't have to cook it. On cool nights we would have a fire in the fireplace and, on occasion, run a movie that the AIRA office would send us occasionally. Unfortunately, those movies too often came one reel at a time, not necessarily in sequence, and we simply gave up on that. The downside of the fireplace was that the ashes and embers fell through a hole in the floor. Occasionally a rat would run up from the hole and scamper across the dining/living room floor. There was a small baseball bat to deal with that problem. Later on, a Raven with more sense than we, devised a sheet metal trap that covered the hole and stopped the rats.

Another interesting, and a bit depressing, resident of our house was a Hmong orphan who roomed with Espi. Lu was about eight and large for a Hmong child, probably our food. Lu had hidden in the jungle when the North Vietnamese entered his small village and massacred the residents in what was a policy of genocide. Lu watched as his parents were killed and he had a number of emotional problems and a real desire for adult attention. Unfortunately, by the end of a typical day of heavy combat flying, dinner at Vang Pao's, and attending the evening CIA meeting few or none of us, including the maintenance guys who also worked long hours, were in much of a mood to play surrogate parent.

Much of our flow of airpower was the F-105 then stationed at Takhli and Korat RTAFB. The flight characteristics of the Thud, particularly its limited turning capability on pull-off, made it more dangerous to us in terms of mid-air collision potential. Once committed to a turn and pulling G, it was difficult to reverse that turn to avoid another aircraft which the Thud pilot might see, or not. Additionally, it was easier for a Thud pilot, without a correcting voice from a back seat to get his pull-off direction confused. On the other hand, many of the pilots were old heads and pretty accurate. Unfortunately, a good deal of the BDA (bomb damage assessment) we gave them at the end of a strike amounted to "100 over 100, NVR (100% or ordnance within 100 meters, no visual results, smoke and foliage). Everybody likes to feel that what they are doing is worthwhile and continually being told 100/100 NVR was not a morale booster.

At one of the nightly CIA meetings they had a bunch of prints of pictures taken after a battle in which a company or so of NVA holed up in a cave and refused to surrender to the larger force of Hmong surrounding the cave entrance. The NVA resorted to a suicide charge in which all of them were killed by torrents of small arms fire. The bodies shown in the pictures were riddled with bullet holes and the CIA base chief asked if we could somehow use these. The bullet holes could be CBU so we decided to send a package of pictures to the F-105 Wing Commander at Takhli. A few days later the Thud pilots were so exuberant during strikes that they were almost difficult to control. We wondered what was going on and found that the Wing Commander, Colonel Mike Horgan, had posted the pictures on about every bulletin board on the base with one caption under each picture – "100/100 NVR". That would undoubtedly be heavily frowned upon today – and perhaps then – but it certainly had the intended effect.

Dan Berry got attention in two ways. One came one day from small arms fire that impacted his right fuel tank a couple of feet from his head. While that certainly got his attention, what got it even more was

CHAPTER FIVE

that the self-sealing tanks were not sealing and he was streaming fuel. Fortunately, he had enough to get back to Long Tieng.

The second source of attention was from the rest of us. Dan, formerly a C-130 pilot, thought that doing acrobatics was great fun although that is not something you can do with a C-130. Now it apparently appeared to him that this was his big chance to do acro. We discovered that he was routinely doing acrobatics in the O-1s we had at Long Tieng. All of us pointed out that there were a number of reasons why this was not a good idea, beyond the reality that acrobatics in the O-1 is not fun in any sense and a sloppy barrel roll was about all in its repertoire. We tried explaining to him that the airplane was not built for acro, that they already had a lot of stress on them, that the airplanes were others' rejects and were not in very good shape, and that we would be flying airplanes that he might have over-stressed which put us in peril, not him. He laughed and grinned and promised not to do that anymore, and of course he did continue. After a couple of months he found the stress of operations in Laos to be too much and he returned to Vietnam. Years later I learned that he was in a rental Cessna 172 flying over Los Angeles and proceeded to do some acro. He pulled the wings off and crashed on a freeway, undoubtedly screwing up rush hour on a grand scale.

The fighter/attack aircraft that we worked consisted of F-105 from Korat and Takhli RTAFB; F-4D from Udorn; F-4E from Korat starting in May 1969; A-1 from Nakhon Phanom RTAFB; and one Navy A-6 flight. We did not work the RLAF T-28D except under very unusual circumstances. They worked on their own at the direction of Vang Pao and were known as the "A team". There was one more piece to the equation and that consisted of Thai Air Force contract pilots flying RLAF T-28D, referred to as the "B team" (there were occasional excursions by the USAF instructors at Det 1, referred to as the "Super B team").

The B team had been created by the early Air Commando types when the RLAF was just beginning to grow to resemble an aerial force. The Thai pilots were well paid by Thai standards but they were incredibly difficult and frustrating to work. Their call sign was always "Eagle (color such as Red)" and they always came in a three-ship formation. If you gave them a rendezvous off the Long Tieng TACAN, they would claim none of their TACAN sets worked. If the clouds were broken, they would not descend through a hole to work. If they were shot at, they left. When you were able to work them they would garble transmissions, fly away from the directions given by the Raven, and generally turn the whole process into a frustrating and time-consuming chaos. I spent one maddening 45 minutes working one of these flights whose results for the day was wounding one friendly soldier. This got me a severe scowl from VP that night. The B team must have complained at some point because we got a message that one of the conditions in their contract was that they could not be subjected to ground fire. That was one hell of an impossible deal! One wonders in what universe that contract was written.

At that time the RLAF did operate from Long Tieng, and Moung Soui which was about 25 miles north, but not on a permanent official basis. Moung Soui was a long laterite runway, perhaps 5000 feet long, that was also the location for a small uniformed US Army advisory team that was a minor illustration of the complexity of the 1962 Geneva Accords. The Army advisors were uniformed because they were advising the rightist neutralists and not the Royal Lao government. There were also leftist neutralists and, of course, the Communist Pathet Lao. This US Army outpost had been attacked a couple of months previously and had taken casualties.

The leader of the Hmong pilots was a remarkable individual named Lee Lue who was, as I recall, a son-in-law of Vang Pao. He always spent the night at Long Tieng, even if his wingmen went elsewhere, and I saw him at VP's dinner most nights. The Royal Lao government, always nervous about coup potential, did not authorize eight T-28Ds, almost all flown by Hmong, to be permanently based at Long Tieng until May. In the meantime, they would often refuel and rearm at Moung Soui – closer to the targets VP wanted them to strike. The USAF would haul fuel and ordnance there for that purpose. This would cease in May. The Hmong flew an exhausting and dangerous six to eight sorties a day each – always led by Lee Lue who was a truly superb pilot.

I was at Moung Soui one day, refueling myself, and pointed out to Lee Lue that there was a NVA PT-76 tank wandering around on the PDJ – the tank crew having to be drunk or insane to do that. I took off to go work near LS- 50 and Lee Lue took off solo behind me. I watched him as he approached the area where I had seen the tank, watched him roll into a 90 degree vertical dive, watched a single bomb depart his T-28, and watched the tank disappear in a huge explosion as the bomb impacted the turret. It wasn't luck, it was pure skill honed by thousands of combat sorties.

Lee Lue would end a typical day by landing at Long Tieng and shutting down his T-28 in a small ramp area across from where we parked on the other side of the runway. The sun would be near setting, long blue-purple shadows lengthening over the airplane and Ly Lue and the crowd that formed. He would sit there, collecting himself from yet another day of constant danger and constant stress, knowing full well that this moment in time could not go on forever. Finally, one of the men in the crowd would climb up onto the wing and help Lee Lue unstrap and climb out of the cockpit, his legs shaking from cramped muscles from a day of ruddering his airplane through certain destruction to another evening landing in that deep and shadowed valley. We would meet at dinner at Vang Pao's, talk a bit, nod our mutual understanding that he indeed represented the motto of those pilots – "Fly until you die".

I had been there about three weeks when I started discerning the different effect my new environment was having on me in contrast to where I had been. In Vietnam I would become extremely focused on what I was doing and on the environment if circumstances demanded it – which they usually did not. I was there, I was engaged, but there was also a thin transparent veneer between me and events most of the time. This was not the case in Northern Laos and there were, I was discovering, a number of factors that made things different and intense beyond anything I had ever experienced.

Among those factors, of course, was the sheer number of airstrikes conducted in an environment that demanded complete concentration regarding terrain, weather, and defenses, and the ground tactical situation. In Vietnam I had controlled a mere 36 airstrikes in six months, compared to 75 my first month in Laos. Another significant element was the knowledge and concentration of the CIA personnel who fully understood and practiced the concepts of teamwork and cooperation at the operational level. Another major influence was the dedication of the Hmong in what was a bloody battle for survival that had marginal long term odds for a favorable outcome – and yet they gave all.

The sum of all these influences seemed to be gradually pushing me through what sometimes seemed to be mental membrane into a different sort of environment, perhaps akin to Alice passing through the looking glass. The mortar attack incident in Vietnam had happened once but now the same phenomena were becoming normal. I became much more situationally aware, much more attuned to following observational clues, and much more sensitive to impending events. When something tells you to turn right now, and you do, and a line of flak goes through where you would have been, you know you have passed through the looking glass. It is a mental state that does wear you down over time.

CHAPTER FIVE

One of the interesting places we visited was LS-46, about 70 miles almost due east of Long Tieng. My procedure for getting there was to fly east for about 45 minutes, turn right at an unusual river junction, and proceed south going east around a large karst formation, and there you were. The elevation was 2900 feet with a 1200 foot clay strip running to the north. When you touched down on the beginning of the strip, what seemed like excessive airspeed got eliminated by a quick upslope near the end. If you were really too fast you would fall off a steep cliff into a canyon. Two case officers were assigned there during the day and usually one was present. I would occasionally stop there to get a verbal update on what they were doing and what was going on in the local area. It seemed a bit odd to sit a comfortable hootch with copies of Field and Stream magazine lying around and having a cup of coffee. Supply, as in many places, was done by dropping cargo. I was there one day when a Continental C-46 (a World War II transport somewhat common in Asia at the time) came by to drop double-sacked rice from a few hundred feet. While I knew Continental and Air America were experts at this it made me very uncomfortable to hear the string of giant thumps as the rice hit the ground. I think the sacks weighed a hundred pounds, certainly enough to flatten my O-1 should it get hit. Unfortunately that day the village idiot ran to catch a rice sack and succeeded. It was educational to watch the locals brushing the rice from the broken bag away from his pulverized body so they could save as much as possible.

An adjacent site, LS-236, some 25 miles northwest, was also worked by the same two case officers. One of them asked me to pick him up there one day so I found the place and was convinced that it would be an easy landing and take-off because there was an Air America Caribou parked there. If I'd had a site book showing LS details, I wouldn't have tried that. What gave me confidence was the presence of the Caribou.

MEETING STEVE CANYON

In Vietnam, at considerably lower elevations, the presence of a Caribou meant that I would have no problem landing and taking-off in my O-1. Two realities totally escaped me at LS–236. The first was that the elevation was probably pretty high, reducing the O-1 takeoff performance. The second was that Air America pilots flew their aircraft, whatever they might be, to the absolute limits of the aircraft capabilities which was not the case most of the time in Vietnam.

I made a good landing on the 1100 foot grass strip running uphill. As I shut down I was horrified to see that the elevation was 4700 feet. A quick look at the performance data in the checklist showed that taking off would be pretty dicey. On the other hand, there was a cliff at the end of the runway in the take-off direction. It was a couple of hundred feet down to some rice paddies and I figured, sort of, that I could make it. I loaded the case officer in back and I used every inch of runway they had, hurtling over the cliff, and staggering across the rice paddies for a while. I told him we wouldn't be going back to LS–236.

April 29 was another normal, busy, day until the end. I had rearmed and refueled at LS-46 and was heading home when Dan Davis described a bad tactical situation at Xieng Khoung, and he was out of fuel. He gave me a quick run-down and departed as I arrived.

Three hundred friendlies were advancing, steadily line abreast, from the ruined town towards a large karst formation. Beyond that was a smaller karst formation, and beyond that the entrance to a large cave. Behind the first karst formation were two BTR-40 Soviet armored personnel carriers, each sporting twin 14.5mm heavy MG -- easily enough to wipe out the friendlies who wouldn't get on the radio and seemed oblivious. Late in the afternoon, the descending sun cast very sharp shadows across the valley floor. It was almost impossible to see objects in shadow unless you descended into the shadow itself -- down to about 500' AGL

CHAPTER FIVE

in this case. The ghost of John Bach was tapping me on the shoulder. On one of these swoops a 37mm near the BTR 40 opened up -- hosing away from a slant range of less than a thousand feet. To make things more interesting, large numbers of enemy troops on the cliffs above the cave began shooting down at my O-1. Scar, my backseater, went to work trying to contact Lee Leu.

Lee Lue showed a few minutes later and led his flight of three T-28Ds in strafing and rocketing the enemy on the cliffs. I gave him general direction on VHF while coaching in a single F-4 released by a fast Fac. Lee Lue worked in a clockwise pattern on the cliff tops while LINCOLN came down the long valley leading from the PDJ to Xieng Khoung. The 37mm whacked away and everyone was taking huge volumes of small arms fire. We were on borrowed time in a situation like this. LINCOLN, inexplicably, dropped 300 meters short from low altitude. The friendlies, inexplicably, kept advancing.

BOBIN, two F-105, checked in and lead's tone of voice said the old pro was there. BOBIN was in at 1725 progressing up the valley at some 500 knots indicated, more than 800 feet per second. The slowness of time in combat made it seem like he was crawling through the shadows and dust and slashing white light. The wait was excruciating, the bad guys couldn't miss me forever. Rolling in to mark at minimum range when BOBIN was a few seconds out was the only option left. The light-dark contrast was extremely disorienting, and must have been far worse for BOBIN at his speed. Pulling off left, down at about 200 feet, the ground and raw slashes of cliff were terrifyingly close. There were an overwhelming sense of ZPU or 37mm rounds about to shatter the Bird Dog into slivers of old aluminum. I looked left in time to see BOBIN skip two Mark 84 (2000 pounders). Two tons of steel and explosive ricocheted gracefully off the valley floor in a gentle arc that ended at the base of the karst where the enemy was hiding. The two APC, the 37mm, and the bad guys disappeared in a shattering blast of smoke and fire. Karst limestone chips rained down in a valley stunned to silence. Scar and I were quiet as we headed home, another day leading to the next.

It was my turn to take an O-1 to Udorn for periodic maintenance and a night off from what had become normal routine. I stopped in Vientiane on the way to drop off some paperwork and was startled to see two odd-looking old airline type airplanes parked at Wattay airport. I learned that they were among the few surviving Boeing Stratoliners originally built in the late 1930s. That was pretty amazing. It was even more astounding to learn that they were the transport means for the International Control Commission (ICC), formed as part of the 1954 French Indochina cease-fire and composed of Canadian, Polish, and Indian military representatives whose job was to assure that the 1954 agreement was not violated. It was definitely a head-shaking moment.

I arrived at Udorn by late afternoon, handed the airplane over to Air America, and headed to the other side of the base for the first episode of what became a ritual. After getting a haircut – something you definitely did not get at Long Tieng – I had a facial. While that sounds odd it did two things for me besides the obvious. One was that it was relaxing and I needed some of that. Another was that it helped extract the last of red Vietnam highland dust from my skin. Our houseboys probably wondered who kept giving them red streaked towels to wash. Then I went to the Officers Club and had a banana split. Then it was time for a few scotches in the bar that was open 24 hours a day. While sitting at the teak bar in the dim light I thought about the last month and its intensity. I had worked 75 air strikes, experienced huge flying challenges, and had succeeded. I went downtown to the Charoen, the best hotel in town, and rewarded myself.

CHAPTER FIVE

Our O-1F at Gia Nghia

The ALO/FAC jeep at the gate to the Advisory Team 32 compound

Burr Smith (center), Vang Pao two to his left,
Long Tieng Valley background.

Long Tieng run way end. VP house at the lower left.
CIA and Raven houses are left of the karst.

CHAPTER FIVE

Long Tieng runway, picture taken in 1971 or 1972.

Fly until you die. Ly Lue on the right.

MEETING STEVE CANYON

Floyd has a beer or two, or three. (Photo courtesy of Ed Lauffer)

Air America loading troops on the
Plain of Jars. (Photo courtesy of Ed Lauffer)

CHAPTER FIVE

Karl Polifka (foreground) and Bob Dunbar on the
PDJ (courtesy of the John Garrity collection)

Raven O-1 in Laos.

MEETING STEVE CANYON

RLAF T-28D at Long Tieng, identical to Raven T-28D.

CHAPTER SIX

In late April there were a couple of examples of the sort of intelligence support and direction that was available from the customer. The first of these was described as an agent report that identified a cave on the central PDJ that contained 500 barrels of fuel. The cave entrance, three by five meters, faced the northwest and was masked with trees. That was the sort of information that went into your hip pocket for use when you got to it. The second piece of information was far more complex.

The Hmong had been gradually forced back by NVA pressure, some of which resulted in major battles in which significantly important Lima Sites were lost. One of these battles, prior to my time, had been at LS-36 which was north of Ban Ban valley towards Sam Nuea which was defined as the "Communist capitol of Laos". The loss of LS-36 was a severe blow to CIA and particularly to Vang Pao who took some time to recover. In the sloping mountains west of Ban Ban was another critically important site, LS-32, some 20 miles southwest of LS-36. A Lieutenant NVA regimental operations officer had defected and revealed in his debriefing the plans of his regiment to take LS-32 with a series of attacks from the north and west. The operations officer detailed the rough locations of his former regiment (some 3000 strong) and the general intended timing of the assaults. He also indicated that, unlike previous NVA attacks, there would be no open door through which the friendly troops and their families could escape. All were to be killed, a condition that certainly steeled the resolve of those at LS-32. The customer, Vang Pao, and the Ravens quickly worked out tactics that we thought would work to counter this attack. We didn't have a lot of time.

The general idea was to deploy small units towards where the NVA forces were supposed to be, engage the NVA in a firefight but from a reasonable aerial ordnance safe-distance while a Raven and airpower was available. Once the NVA were engaged it was difficult for them to maneuver and the ensuing airstrike caused considerable casualties in a brief period of time, usually in fifteen to twenty minutes. An additional advantage to us was that the NVA, once committed to a plan of action, rarely deviated from that plan even when it was obvious that things were not going as forecast.

The strikes against this regiment went on for over a week but it was difficult to impossible to actually see results. In the same time frame I checked out another new guy, Mike Cavanaugh. One visible indicator that things were not going well for the NVA came early one morning when I made a low pass over LS-32 and its trench and bunker network. The much-weakened NVA had attempted their classic night human wave assault. There were piles of NVA bodies stacked around the site while the friendlies had taken few casualties. One group of NVA had occupied an outlying bunker, futilely blazing away at anything they could see. I worked a flight of F-105 on the bunker and it disappeared. This was the end of the operation for the NVA. Communications intercepts indicated that they had lost much of that regiment, mostly to air strikes.

During episodes such as the LS-32 battle the Ravens that were airborne, a minimum of two at any one time, would also work other requirements throughout our area, brokering the use of the incoming air

CHAPTER SIX

between ourselves over FM radio. Those other requirements included support for troops at other LS, attacks on supply dumps (real, not suspected), and interdiction of transport along the road structure, primarily Route 7 which came in from North Vietnam and threaded through Ban Ban valley to the PDJ.

One day I was flying along Route 7 in Ban Ban valley, a very dangerous place, with Scar in the back seat. He was dozing when I ran one fuel tank dry, resulting in the engine quitting. This was normally no big deal, you just switched over to the other tank and the engine started immediately. It was part of a technique to know how much fuel you actually had since the float gauges were not reliable. Scar, of course, was instantly awake and looked out the window and saw we were over Ban Ban. "Berry, berry bad," he said, "many, many enemy". True but not a problem except that the engine didn't start and we were losing altitude fairly quickly. Scar tightened his seat harness, having survived several crashes, and had a very worried look on his face. The look on my face probably matched his as I quickly ran through engine start procedures. There was no ground fire but you could sense a thousand sets of eyes watching our descent towards a very unpleasant death. A few hundred feet above the valley floor the engine started and we departed as quickly as possible, leaving a disappointed enemy behind.

Some aspects of our environment were changing, as is always the case in life itself. One of these changes was the increased presence of what were called "fast FAC". These were F-4 from Udorn (call sign "LAREDO") and Korat (call sign "TIGER"). These were a follow-on to the original fast FAC program that flew F-100 (call sign "Misty") and worked strikes against selected and recognizable targets in southern North Vietnam. This made perfect sense given the lethality of the air defenses there and the lack of consequences if the target selected by 7th Air Force happened to be of little or no importance. It made far less sense in our environment for several reasons.

The military situation in Northern Laos was complex in that friendly forces were scattered over a wide area and operated in small groups throughout that area. We didn't know where every Hmong unit was at any given moment and 7th Air Force certainly had no idea nor did any F-4 pilot living 100+ miles away. Friendly villages were also scattered over a wide area and from time to time might have an enemy presence near or in them. That didn't mean they were enemy locations. Unfortunately, the presence of an NVA truck tire track in a village meant, to an Air Force imagery interpreter and the command hierarchy, that the village was "enemy". We later learned that such locations were then put on a target list and fast FAC authorized to strike such places. There was never any attempt by 7th Air Force to verify the validity of these designations with those who knew reality. If this sounds like South Vietnam pre-plans, it was the same level of thinking. At the same time, we learned from a source within 7th Air Force that any reporting we made was disregarded because it was "tainted" by our association with the CIA.

Another aspect of the fast FAC program was the ego issue. Moving from being an ordinary fighter pilot in any given fighter wing to being a fast FAC in that same wing was a major step up the recognition scale. It was prestigious, it was a recognition of superior flying and thinking skills (at least in theory), and it was career enhancing. Many, perhaps most, fighter pilots had significant egos. Becoming a fast FAC often boosted that personality characteristic to a level at which self-doubt was uncommon. It is fairly rare in such situations for the chosen ones, so to speak, to challenge or disregard the direction and guidance provided by the organization that had raised their standing – and yet some did, to their credit.

CHAPTER SIX

In retrospect it would seem that introducing a fast FAC program in Northern Laos allowed 7th Air Force to exert their will around the existing arrangements that had excluded their direct authority over use of much of the airpower they generated. That thought is reinforced by the contents of the unpublished "History of the War in Northern Laos", written by the Office of Air Force History, in which the Embassy/CIA methods of employing airpower are consistently attacked as being inefficient and ineffective.

The reality was that we were supporting a large CIA operation authorized by the President of the United States. The CIA was well aware of the many nuances of the environment where they were operating, had good intelligence sources, and shared that information with the Ravens as necessary to accomplish the mission defined by the United States Government. Additionally, many of the CIA personnel had many years of experience in Southeast Asia and provided exceptionally valuable insights otherwise not available. In short, the CIA provided the requirements for the use of airpower, and provided essential information – often in near real time -- to make that airpower use exceptionally useful and effective. The Ravens were experienced professionals who implemented that airpower selectively and effectively.

The United States Air Force, in contrast, was focused on their basic doctrine of centralized control, decentralized execution which translated into a single airpower manager at the peak of a pyramid making all decisions regarding the use of airpower on specific targets which they either generated, in a multi-day process, or otherwise approved. This operational concept was superb if applied to the World War II strategic bombing campaigns – from which this doctrine originated. The concept did not work well in an environment of mostly fleeting targets, constantly shifting tactical situations, and multiple layers of shifting semi-transparent political and military factions. Part of the Air Force attitude probably resulted from a bitter doctrinal fight they had with the Army a few years previously. Looking, in Air Force eyes, like you were providing "flying artillery" came a bit too close to resembling the Army. Lastly, few Air Force members had useful experience in Southeast Asia compared to CIA, among others. Constantly attempting to force the duplication in Laos, or Vietnam, of a process that was unproductive beyond its original World War II environment was never the path to military success. Far too many in this chain chose, either through ignorance or self-promotion, to not challenge the status quo in any way or for any reason.

Another change was the introduction of the F-4E to Korat. Almost all of the F-4 we worked came from Udorn and were the D model. Many of the aircrew at Udorn had been recently checked out in the airplane. The rest of the fast-movers we had been working were F-105 from Korat and Takhli. The F-4E gradually replaced the Thuds at Korat. What made the F-4E different, beyond improvements made to the airplane, was the very high experience level of the crews at that time. This became awesomely obvious to me when I worked SCUBA, an F-4E two-ship on some bunkers and hootches in the PDJ area. The normal standard load for an F-4 was 12 Mark 82 (500 pound) slicks and 3 cans of CBU 24. Most of the F-4 flights we worked would take most or all of that bomb load to destroy the equivalent of ten houses. A two-ship would carry, obviously, double that load but would still use all the bombs for a simple job. Bomb releases were normally done as "trips", three bombs per pass. The CBU was used elsewhere in situations like this.

After Scuba checked in and I got the target briefed, lead asked if I wanted them to drop singles. That would mean 24 passes for which I didn't have the time and an exhibition that would attract more ground fire. My reply was to go trips and I marked the target area. Lead dropped three Mark 82 and, whump, the target was gone! Oops, hold 'em high and dry while I find something else. Okay, mark, two's in, whump, target gone! Over and over they hit targets with incredible precision. A new something for us to keep in mind – have multiple targets in the area when these guys show up! The drama count would go up considerably with time.

This account leads to the occasional question of which type of aircraft was best at delivering ordnance? I worked 495 airstrikes in Laos, and 36 in Vietnam, involving six types of aircraft and my response would be that the real answer was the pilot, not the airplane. Some people will say that the A-1 with its large and varied bomb load and slow speed was the most accurate. On the other hand, the worst bombing errors I observed were done by A-1 pilots. Some people will say that the F-4 was mediocre at best, but Scuba represented a class not of airplane but of pilot. That hackneyed old phrase that practice makes perfect, is true.

Relations between the AIRA office and the Ravens, at least the Long Tieng Ravens, had been a bit prickly for some time. The main troublemakers had departed, at least for now, so most of us were invited to the AIRA staff house for a late afternoon cocktail party. After spending the night we would fly back to Long Tieng at first light to get back to work. The cocktail party went fairly well until, as the sun was setting, I asked the admin officer where we were going to sleep. His reply helped me understand some of the friction that existed. "I guess you can sleep on the floor," was his reply. I held him by the neck and lifted him off the floor with one hand, which shows what you can do when you're pissed off. They were playing their oh-so-secret game and said we had to stay there. We all left and went to various places to sleep after visiting the White Rose and Les Rendezvous des Amis (aka Lulu's).

MEETING STEVE CANYON

We had run into some fighter pilots at Udorn who thought that 37mm was no threat since they were fast and it was a World War II era weapon. Someone got the idea that perhaps if we gave a fighter wing an operable 37mm they could play games on it and see how easy it was to track aircraft and, hopefully, understand, that it doesn't take high tech to kill you. We decided that the F-105 wing at Takhli would be our first recipient since they did consistently good work. The customer cleaned up a captured 37mm and flew the gun and me to Takhli in an Air America C-123. Much as I tried, I got few Thud pilots to play games with the 37mm, a learning experience ignored. They put a fence around it and made it into a museum piece.

I spent my time in the bar telling stories and getting myself set up for a ride in the venerable Thud the next day. The Thud had been the primary attack airplane during the Rolling Thunder operation over North Vietnam, and had borne the brunt of the losses. Eventually, over half of the F-105 produced would be lost in combat. One joke was that an optimist was a heavy smoker Thud pilot who thought he'd die of lung cancer.

I enjoyed my brief time at Takhli and found much less of the arrogance too often present elsewhere. Aside from the ride in the F-105 the next day, one very memorable experience was leaving the Officer's Club and walking to the hootch where I would sleep. Outside the club there was an open field that had perhaps once been a parade ground but was now covered with knee-high grass. My hootch was on the other side of the field but I was advised to walk down the middle of the road that ran around the field. The reason? The field was full of cobras. I later knew a tanker pilot who had gotten fairly smashed at the Takhli club a couple of times and had walked directly across that field in the dark. The third night he walked out and saw numerous guys sweeping flashlights in the

CHAPTER SIX

field. There were scores of waist-high moving pairs of reflected light – cobras. He went back and had another drink.

The next day I got in the back of a two seat Thud and took off for a mission to Northern Laos. We had an uneventful time while being directed by my roommate Dan Davis who got fairly confused when I started talking to him. On the way back we separated from lead and I got to fly for a while. I started a barrel roll at 400+ knots indicated and the pilot immediately started to caution me. I completed the roll but we burbled on the edge of a stall all the way around. The Thud had very high wing loading (aircraft weight divided by the wing square footage) as did all aircraft ever built by Republic and I could now better appreciate the maneuvering difficulties they faced during an airstrike.

I was standing near base operations waiting for a hop to Bangkok when the wing commander's car was driven past with the Chief of Staff of the USAF in the back seat with the wing commander. General Ryan pointed at me, the guy in the black flight suit, and I could see Colonel Horgan explaining things. I spent a couple of days in the hectic intensity of Bangkok and was glad to get home to Long Tieng where things were more orderly and predictable, in a way. The next day I worked nine airstrikes in heavy ground fire. The new normal.

We had two new guys – Ed Lauffer who had arrived from Bao Lac just south of me in Vietnam, and Grif Quinby who was an Air Force flight surgeon who would be with us for six months. Medical treatment for us was not the primary purpose for Grif's presence, it was getting the shell of a local hospital functioning and improving the lot of the locals. He was perfect for the job in that he, like us, was oriented towards results and not rules. Within a couple of days of Grif's arrival we were sitting on our screened in porch drinking Johnnie Walker Black ($3.25 per 40 ounce bottle), watching the setting sun shadow the valley, and talking about our childhoods. Grif's father had been a public health doctor in Montgomery, Alabama right after World War II. My father had been an Air Force Colonel stationed at Maxwell AFB just outside Montgomery at the same time. It turned out that Grif and I were in the same ten member first grade class at Hurt Military Academy (there wasn't much military about it). We have remained in touch ever since.

About sunset one day Ed and I were standing on the wooden deck outside our respective rooms when there was a burst of automatic weapons fire fairly nearby. We each instantly reverted to our previous Vietnam experiences and life went into slow motion as we dove into the screen doors of our rooms, rolling on the floor, and snatching our CAR-15 and then repositioning ourselves on the deck. It probably took six seconds but it seemed an eternity. We were laying spread about 90 degrees apart, and silently scanning the hill behind us, weapons ready. I motioned to Ed and he nodded as I silently lurched forward and bent over the deck edge at the waist, Ed holding my ankles. I checked the underside of our house and Ed pulled me back. After perhaps ten minutes and no activity, we parked our weapons and went to our bar. Two of the maintenance guys were in an adjoining room and said they saw what we had been doing, and decided that opening their door would have been a bad idea. Very true!

During World War II there was a subset of the British Special Operations Executive (SOE) known as Force 136 operating out of then Ceylon, now Sri Lanka. While most of their operations involved indigenous people in larger Asian countries, there was a small effort that operated in Northern Laos. I became familiar with that bit of history when a Thai architect, accompanied by his incredibly beautiful wife, visited so he could do a site survey for the expansion of our existing house and a new adjoining house since we were getting more and more people. We were

CHAPTER SIX

having a drink on a terrace behind the CIA house, soon to be an enclosed bar, when I asked him where he had gone to architecture school. His reply was "Ohio State". I was taken back a bit and asked him how he had come to go to Ohio State. "GI Bill," he smiled, "I jumped into this valley with Force 136." I was impressed.

In the latter part of May we experienced first-hand with blinding clarity what we had mostly left behind in Vietnam. A rather porky photo interpreter (PI) arrived with a target list whose entries we were supposed to strike with the extra 240 sorties in three days that would be provided by 7th Air Force. It became very obvious very quickly that we were, for the most part, back to the dreaded Montagnard footpath intersection sort of thinking, This time, however, a lot of the listed "targets" were Hmong footpath intersections. Amongst us we agreed that we would strike what seemed to be reasonable targets on the list (a few) and simply run a line of strafe through the rest, thereby "striking" it. We would then use the extra air on the significant backlog of targets that we hadn't yet hit. The porky PI was delighted with the (mostly phony) results as he ate our food at an incredible rate. Many years later I read in the Air Force "History of the War in Northern Laos" that this exercise was called "Operation Stranglehold" and was a stunning success. Yes it was, but not because of 7th Air Force and their thin knowledge.

I had been at Long Tieng long enough to perceive some differences between Ravens in the way they interacted with our reality. We all did the same job, although we each used different techniques and approaches to any given situation. Giving direction while running an airstrike dictated that the FAC be in a certain common altitude/distance-from-target block for the practical reasons of constantly observing the target area and avoiding the strike aircraft. Having said all that, I seemed to take less ground fire than others, although I certainly took plenty. This was demonstrated somewhat dramatically not long after Mike Cavanaugh arrived. I worked a couple of strikes around Xieng Khoung one morning. There was some small arms fire for the hour or so I was around the town, but not too much. Cavanaugh relieved me, asking about the ground fire. A few minutes later I heard him on the radio, ". . . I'm getting tired of this shit . . .". I turned in my seat to see his O-1 surrounded by 12.7 mm tracers. Whatever kind of magic I had, it was real and stayed with me through this tour and then another flying the RF-4. Again, I cannot explain it but it is real.

LS-184 was about 80 miles north of Long Tieng, and almost 20 miles south of the North Vietnamese border. We went there periodically but it was more of a presence declaration than any truly urgent need. One day I was working a target just west of LS-184 with two F-105. Once again, lead's voice declared him to be the old head while two's voice indicated he was, well, number two. After I briefed what I wanted them to do, two told lead that the light on the combining glass of his sight had failed – what should he do? Lead's reply showed his experience in the Thud. He told two to make a 30 degree dive on the target and release at 3000 feet above ground level at 500 knots indicated. He should eyeball the top edge of the combining glass and align it with the end of the pitot boom that stuck out the nose of the Thud and have that lined up on the target as he released. If you are a pilot you will understand that this is a lot easier to say, and write, than it is to do, especially the first time. This, I thought, would be interesting. I wasn't concerned about any gross errors since there weren't any friendlies around. Two rolled in on my mark which still lingered on that windless day. Four Mark 82 arced off the Thud in a ballistic descent that, yes, obliterated my mark. This was a demonstration of true piloting skill. I suggested that maybe they ought to remove the light bulbs in all their combining glasses.

CHAPTER SIX

Don Service, our senior guy, worked a flight of F-105 on a cave mouth on the Southeastern PDJ. The flight had some "Bullpup" air-to-ground (AGM) wire guided missiles which they punched into the cave. The Bullpup was a little scary since it would periodically go unguided and no one knew where it would go. After one almost drilled me I made sure I was behind the fighters using it. Dumping ordnance into caves, even if you don't have hard evidence that there is anything there, was usually a good idea since the enemy used many of the very large number of caves for supply dumps and troop billeting. In this case, nothing happened and Don finished up the strike and flew away. About 45 minutes later I flew past the cave and saw the mouth gushing smoke and flames. Getting on FM I found out who had run the strike and told Don what was going on. As I was circling and talking a village about a mile away suddenly erupted in flames and then exploded! Ah, a long cave connection indeed. The place burned and exploded for over 12 hours as observed by Hmong teams in the nearby hills.

Don Service was doing a fine job but fate intervened via kidney stones so he had to leave Long Tieng for repairs and then finish out his time at another site. He was replaced by Walt Ackerlund, another Thud pilot who had been at some other site. Walt quickly adapted to the increased tempo and intensity of Long Tieng.

June started with a sort of Alice-in-Wonderland experience involving the rightest neutralists and their US Army advisors at Moung Soui (L-108). Major NVA units had moved westward from the LS-32 area and there were now several battalions in the hills to the northeast of Moung Soui. The rightest-neutralist infantry battalions were supported by a Thai artillery battalion. Vang Pao had asked us to visit the neutralists and cooperate with them as much as possible given the threatening position of the NVA. Should Moung Soui fall the enemy would be only about 25 miles north-north west of Long Tieng. The NVA would also be in a position to move westward by road to Route 13, the north-south road that connected Vientiane and Luang Prabang, the Royal capitol.

I sat next to the neutralist commander in a tent while one of his subordinates briefed me on the current situation. The commander had the physical appearance of an upper class lowland Lao with light colored skin. The briefing was straight out of the US Army playbook with the briefer standing very erect to the side of a briefing board that had 1:50000 maps of the area covered with acetate sheets on which enemy positions were marked. The briefer's pointer flashed up and down as he went through the NVA order of battle. It was impressive and very professional looking. I told the commander that I would soon have several airstrikes inbound and we agreed which place to strike first. At the conclusion of the first strike he assured me that his troops would attack into what would a badly battered NVA unit. I took off feeling very positive and confident that we were going to do a real job on the NVA. The time from takeoff to the strike area was about three minutes.

METRIC, a flight of four F-105, started the show at 1430 by hammering one NVA position for 15 minutes. I observed eight bunkers destroyed and at least 6 KBA (killed by air) although there were undoubtedly more. The next flight wasn't due for a half hour and I hoped that the friendlies didn't get stuck in something bad during that time. I needn't have worried since the friendlies did not move an inch. I quickly returned to Moung Soui and talked to the commander again. My contact with the commander did not involve arm-waving on my part but I was certainly insistent that he had to take advantage of the opportunity provided by a heavy airstrike. He agreed but seemed a bit embarrassed.

MACHETE, four F-4E, started working at 1519 and continued for 21 minutes. They were followed a few minutes later by NEWARK, four

CHAPTER SIX

F-105, who continued pounding selected areas for 15 minutes. In the BDA, among other items, was a 12.7 mm that had been firing at me and the fighters, and two 82mm recoilless rifles. The friendlies didn't do anything. I landed and talked to the Neutralist commander, pointing out that the Americans had delivered 39 tons of ordnance in a bit over 90 minutes and that they had done nothing. I went on to say, way over my pay grade, that we weren't going to do any more close air support unless he was actually going to engage the enemy. My hope was that this would prompt the commander to do something besides sit and watch.

I went over all this with the customer and they pointed out that for both military and political reasons it would be wise to have Vang Pao use the eight RLAF T-28, under Ly Lue's direction, work with the neutralists. In the next five days the RLAF T-28 delivered 100 tons of ordnance, 400 x 500 pound bombs, on the NVA, causing more serious damage to their capabilities. The Neutralists did not attack and airpower alone was not going to make the NVA go away. This would evolve into a very bad situation in the next month.

We often would carry a box of C rations under the front seat in the O-1 and stop some where to have lunch. One day I landed at Moung Soui and there was no one around when I got out and perched myself on a fuel drum to begin my not-so-attractive lunch. About that time a Hmong kid sidled up looking for a handout. The Hmong were fairly protein-poor so sharing the "spiced beef" C ration would not be a problem, particularly since I didn't much care for the "spiced beef". I opened the can of peaches and ate half, giving the kid the rest. I did the same with the ancient bread. Then I opened the can of spiced beef with its quarter inch of congealed fat on top, poled it around a bit, and handed the can to the kid. He looked at the can, looked at me with disgust, tossed the

MEETING STEVE CANYON

can over his shoulder and walked away. Maybe I should have related this experience to whoever made this stuff.

While my couple of months in Laos had been pretty intense, particularly in comparison to Gia Nghia, things seem to be acquiring more of an edge as June progressed. I, and I assume the other Ravens, were getting more sustained fuel and ammunition fires and explosions and ground fire seemed to be picking up. On June 12th I flew our U-17 far north to LS-184 for their periodic support and a relative bit of tension relief since that area was relatively quiet, I thought.

I was carrying an unusual backseater in the four seat U-17 that day. He was a former site commander who had burned out in that position and had now been assigned the relatively safe job of flying around in airplanes that got shot at a lot. That should give you some perspective about the relative stress of being in the infantry. He seemed to be a nice guy and climbed into the back seat with a handheld VHF radio, rather than sit up front with me in the side-by-side cockpit. He didn't speak a word of English. We chugged up to LS-184, taking a bit less than an hour to get there. I talked with RAINBOW at LS-184 in English and the backseater followed that exchange with one in Hmong on his radio. After drilling around LS-184 for a while I worked two sets of fighters, MARLIN a F-105 two-ship and LOCUST an F-4E two ship. They got a few bunkers, torched some fuel, and got a few NVA. It seemed like a nice easy day as I started heading south. Things were about to change.

The backseater was chattering away with someone in Hmong and then handed me his radio, pointing at the frequency. I tuned VHF to the frequency and started talking to KINGPIN who was at LS-198, some 35 miles northwest of LS-185. He had a severe troops-in-contact situation and I told him we would be there in about 15 minutes. LS-198 was really, really north and less than 40 miles south of Dien Bien Phu in

CHAPTER SIX

North Vietnam. It gave me a kind of eerie feeling. I called Cricket and told them what was going on and that I'd call back when I had a better idea of the situation but I would undoubtedly need some air. One real problem I had was that I was out of WP marking rockets. This was going to be very difficult.

When I got there the situation was worse than I thought it would be. The minimal number of troops assigned to KINGPIN were off to the west of the site on an operation. A few miles to his southeast he had a squad of soldiers in a small trench position in the open on top of a small hill surrounded by a company of NVA who were closing in for an easy kill of some eight or ten Hmong. To make things worse, there were about a thousand civilians at the site with virtually no military protection at the moment.

I called Cricket again and told them that I had a very tight TIC situation and I need a four-ship of F-4E, repeat F-4E. They understood completely. I made several low passes between 50 and 100 feet to get oriented and was immediately sprayed by small arms fire. The site commander in the backseat of hunkered down on the floor. Maybe this flying stuff wasn't such a piece of cake after all.

MACHETE, four F-4E, checked in and I gave them a rundown of the situation including my lack of marking rockets and got their ordnance lineup which was the usual standard load. Where the friendlies were was at the intersection of five modest ridgelines that resembled a starfish in their configuration. The slight valleys created by the starfish ridgelines could give me protection from what I had in mind. I asked Machete to orbit high and dry and keep an eye on me as I passed over the friendlies at perhaps 50 feet. I told Machete that I would rock my wings when I was directly over the friendlies and to keep that position in mind. I then told them that I would make a very low altitude pass over the enemy forces closest to the friendlies and rock my wings where I wanted the first load of Mark 82 trips. This took a great deal of coordination between me and Machete but we quickly got our rhythm.

Each aircraft would call their ordnance release after I rocked my wings and I would dive down into the shallow valleys skimming just above the treetops. The first set of bombs impacted directly on the place, and the troops, that I had intended. And so it went pass after pass by me, and pass by pass by Machete. Most remarkable was their use of the 12 CBU 24 canisters they released.

The minimum safe distance for the use of CBU 24 was 1000 meters. Machete, following my initial designation of the friendly position and my repeated marking passes, made pass after pass dropping single cans of CBU that sparkled across the landscape to within a hundred meters of the friendlies. It was a truly remarkable performance. There was still some ground fire after they had finished dropping their load so I started to roll in once more when Machete lead cautioned me to back off since they saw the muzzle flashes. Each F-4E rolled into multiple passes firing a total of 2400 rounds of 20mm cannon fire at 100 rounds per second. There was no more ground fire and the enemy had been shattered. It took until the next day before I could pass the results on to Machete's headquarters at Korat. In 19 minutes they had wiped out the NVA company. Sixty bodies were found with numerous blood trails indicating, essentially, that there were few survivors. The tension of the day was not yet over.

I headed south for home but was certain I didn't have enough fuel to make it. After a total flight time of 7 hours and 15 minutes, on a fuel capacity of 7 hours, I landed at Moung Soui to refuel to make sure I would make that last mountainous 25 miles. There was only one problem – there were no fresh fuel drums at Moung Soui, everything was empty. I found an empty oil can and cut the top enough to slosh residual fuel from empty barrels in it enough to clean the oil out. Then I rounded up enough empty barrels to eventually give myself about five gallons. My backseater watched, somewhat bemused, at this odd ending to a tough day.

When we got back to Long Tieng I had Larry the radio operator send a query to the AIRA office asking why there was no fuel at Moung Soui. We got a reply that said that Moung Soui was "in imminent danger of being overrun" and that they had terminated fuel supplies. They had failed to tell us and that kind of made one wonder about what kind of thinking went on down there. At the very best one of us could land there out of fuel and be stuck there for a while, where time on the ground equaled vulnerability. One kind of got the drift that we were truly on our own.

The LS-198 site commander was at the evening Vang Pao dinner that night, and it was a time for him to shine and I certainly understood his desire to attain some stature and recognition from VP. He also had my backseater of the day with him and VP publically recognized his contributions to a significant event. I had rarely flown with backseaters for almost a month and while this guy did good work, I did not fly with a backseater again for months. Unfortunately, this particular backseater died two months later when a new Raven crashed on his first solo mission. This was not a forgiving environment.

I had gone to pilot training at Laughlin AFB in Del Rio, Texas. In the advanced jet phase, flying the T-38, I had one instructional ride with a different instructor in our flight. Jim Tulis had a unique New England accent that was unique on the radio. During our out-and-back flight he had suggested I needed to do some fuel transfer which I started but forgot to stop. For this, Jim "pinked" (failed) me on that ride. Late one morning a four ship of F-105 checked in to work a target on the PDJ. Lead's voice was unmistakable – it had to be Jim Tulis. I asked lead if he'd been an IP at Laughlin and he, surprise in his voice, said that he had. My reply was, "You pinked me on a ride, I'll be judging your performance." They did very well.

Near noon one day the weather was marginal with constantly changing, low rapidly moving clouds that broke up later in the day. MANTIS, two F-105, checked in and announced that this was the "champagne flight" for both of them – their last mission – and hoped that I had a good target. I was the only Raven airborne and was over the central PDJ near where the gasoline storage cave was supposed to be. I briefed the target and had them use their bombs to blow down the trees on the northwest side of the little hillock that contained the cave. Sure enough, when they were done with the bombs the entrance was visible. At my direction they pitched their CBU into a nearby tree line and began making very low altitude low angle strafe runs trying to get their cannon fire inside the cave. Nothing happened on their first pass and I was starting to think that perhaps this would be a dud target. Lead pulled off his second pass and two rolled in and started to fire when smoke suddenly gushed out of the cave mouth followed by a massive fireball. Two barely cleared the fireball which had to be at least 250 feet high. The Thud pilots were yelling with enthusiasm and were happy with a BDA report that included 500 barrels of fuel destroyed. I came back to the area several hours later and the fire was so hot that it was pulling low clouds towards the cave and then pushing them up with the rising heat. The fire burned for more than four hours.

Doc Quinby was making steady progress in creating something of a medical system for the Hmong and in equipping the very basic hospital at the southeastern end of the valley. Grif had done some basic training for a couple of Hmong assistants and they lined up the outpatients every morning for Grif to check. This often amounted to several hundred patients a day. One odd thing was the high incidence of goiter, a thyroid gland inflammation. The backseater "Scar" was so named for the surgical scar around his neck when his goiter problem was addressed that way. Making this incidence rate even odder, at least to me, was that iodized salt would make the problem go away. Air America delivered salt to the locals, but not iodized salt. One wonders what the reason for that might have been.

Doc's very modest hospital, extremely primitive by Western standards, was gradually filling with essential equipment and supplies, faster than we thought it would be. Sometime later I discovered why. Grif had approached the base hospital commander, a Colonel, at Udorn. He told the Colonel that he, the Colonel, probably wasn't aware of it but that he had an obligation to support a covert program in Laos with medical equipment and supplies. No, the Colonel replied, he wasn't aware of that but he would be happy to help and so he did. A number of months later the Pacific Air Forces Inspector General team did an inspection of the base. They asked the hospital commander why he was missing $250,000 in equipment and supplies ($1.5 million in 2013 money). Ah, replied the Colonel, it is support for a covert program and I cannot discuss it. It was a great answer, which they would not pursue. When Grif returned to England AFB in Louisiana and got back to being a normal Air Force doctor they got a new hospital commander. Yes, you guessed right.

We also acquired a new Raven 1 when Mel Hart departed in July. Andy Patten was a fighter pilot Lieutenant Colonel with an interesting background and more prone to giving useful advice on a number of subjects without getting pushy. An Australian by birth, Andy had enlisted in the Army Air Forces at the age of 15, he told me, in 1945 because his parents wanted him to have GI Bill benefits. He graduated from Yale and re-entered the Air Force and graduated from pilot training. He was among the first to fly the Air Force version of the F-4.

We also had another arrival at Long Tieng, and a rather puzzling one. Joe Bauer was an Air Force intelligence officer who was one class ahead of me in Officer Training School and lived across the hall there. It made no sense to us, nor to Joe, why we would have an intelligence officer assigned to us except for one possible convoluted reason. It is possible, one supposes, that the Air Force thought that Joe would be a funnel for intelligence support flowing downhill to us rather than us relying on the Central Intelligence Agency whose operations we were supporting. In any event, we got no "intelligence support" from the Air Force and Joe functioned as a clerk reporting our daily BDA summaries. He was later joined by an older Sergeant. I am not sure where everyone was sleeping.

Since I had to physically return to Vietnam to out-process from my TDY (temporary duty) status and get PCS (permanent change of station) orders by the end of June, I asked Walt Ackerlund and Andy Patten if it was okay if I took some leave to Australia after I got done with the annoying paperwork process in Vietnam. They agreed and Andy suggested I visit RAAF (Royal Australian Air Force) station at Williamtown where he had done an exchange tour. It was, I found, an interesting emotional experience to ask to take time off from a very difficult task to which we had all dedicated ourselves – perhaps regret edged with a bit of guilt. On the other hand, I had worked 185 airstrikes in a very difficult environment in about ten weeks and was feeling a little rough around the edges. By about 23 June I dropped an O-1 off at Udorn for overhaul and called our contact at 7th Air Force in Saigon to arrange for a trip to Australia. Technically, we were not eligible for R&R or leave trips on R&R flights. There were, however, always spare spaces reserved for those whose tours were almost over. Chief Master Sergeant Pat Mahoney in Saigon was in a position to lie about us and our status and did so on a regular basis. He set me up for an Australia trip about the 26th of June.

CHAPTER SEVEN

I managed to get back to Nha Trang without too much difficulty and turned in my CAR-15 and .38 pistol which was about all supply cared about. After chatting for a while about the Raven program with the new ops officer I went to the second floor of the CPBO (Central Base Personnel Office) to go through what should have been a simple out-processing exercise. While I was wearing a black unmarked flight suit, I had the necessary orders and presented them to two Airman seated at desks in the mildly sweltering heat made bearable by a couple of electric fans. Sorry, they said, they only did out-processing on Tuesdays so come back next week. I didn't raise my voice but I did press them to the extent that they called the Lt Colonel who was the CBPO chief. The LC said the same thing in a pretty pushy tone and went downstairs and crossed the dirt street to the Officer's Club for lunch.

Looking through the screened window openings towards the Club I wondered what to do next, perhaps seeing what the 21st TASS commander could do. Suddenly, the door to the Club burst open and the CBPO chief charged out and ran across the street, thumped up the stairs and into the room with a mild look of panic on his face. "Out-process him, out-process him", he shouted," get him out of here!" He ran down the stairs and went somewhere. The two Airmen shrugged and I was done in five minutes.

MEETING STEVE CANYON

Since it was lunch time I went over to the Club and there was the 21st TASS ops officer sitting at a table with some other squadron guys. He had a big smile on his face. "Get out-processed?", he asked. "Yeah", I replied, "and damned fast. What was it with the CBPO guy?" The ops officer laughed. The CBPO Lt Colonel had been in charge there for about two weeks when the Inspector General team showed up, the ops officer explained, and blamed him for everything that was screwed up. He had a nervous breakdown and was in the hospital at Cam Ranh for a couple of weeks. "When he came over here today he asked who you were and why you wanted to out-process right now. I told him there was a special unit of very unstable psychopathic killers and you were one of them and that if he wanted to see the sun rise again he better do what you wanted". Well, it worked and that's what counts.

I left Nha Trang that night bound for Saigon on another Scatback T-39. The pilot, yet another starchy Lt Colonel (where did they get all these guys?), berated me for not wearing a uniform. I held my orders about 3 inches from his face so he could read that civilian clothing was permitted. He still didn't get it.

The R&R processing center at Tan Son Nhut Air Base was named Camp Alpha and was run by the Army. I got in rather late, got a bunk, and crashed. In standard Army fashion, we all had to be cleaned up and out of there by 0700 so the maids could work. Sleeping on would have been great since we didn't process until three, but that was not to be. We finally boarded the World Airways Boeing 707 flight to Sydney via Darwin around five. I dozed much of the way until we landed in Darwin at something like 0200 local time. All was well since that part of the trip involved an open bar while they spent an hour refueling the airplane. I think all of us enjoyed every minute of that and we were all a bit spun up as we approached Sydney around dawn. Yet another different experience was unfolding.

CHAPTER SEVEN

The Navy ran the R&R processing location in downtown Sydney and everything took about 20 minutes before they turned us loose to sign up for hotels and tours. I had been advised to go for the hotels desk first and get an R&R rate at the Wentworth, then one of the best in town. It wasn't much of a taxi ride to the hotel and I got some breakfast and a nap before I set out to explore Sydney. A few minutes into that exploration I realized that I had a problem.

I was used to living an intense and dangerous life based in a narrow jungle valley with limited people contact. I could control much of what happened in that life, or avoid things I couldn't control if I must. Now I had escaped from that life but was not at all ready for the endless bustle and noise of a city of several million people pursuing an incalculable number of directions and purposes.

The R&R center, extremely well run, seemed to have noticed this reaction in a lot of people that flowed through their doors. I signed up for a trip to Hayman Island on the Great Barrier Reef. I planeload of 27 of us would depart in the morning on an Ansett Airlines Short-Sunderland flying boat of World War II vintage. While there I talked for a while with a lovely and engaging woman employee, Gillian Davies. We would see each other a number of times and, while nothing significant ever happened, I think we were on each other's radar for a while.

It was almost a thousand miles to Hayman, a good six hours on the lumbering flying boat the likes of which I had last seen in Tahiti when I worked on a schooner in 1957. We were accompanied by some of the R&R contractor employees whose purpose, I think, was to show us around and keep us engaged. There was a considerable supply of liquor on board which we, mostly the pilots, pretty much finished while we talked. When we arrived and went ashore I felt my mental discomfort system slowing down considerably. The R&R center employees were a bit upset when it started raining and kept on raining for almost our entire visit. They organized a lot of Australian style mental games, singing, dancing, and anything to keep us entertained. After the trip was over a number of us were invited to a cocktail party where we sang a song – "It's Raining on Hayman" – set to the tune of "Winchester Cathedral". I think that most of us US types got what we were looking for, a bridge to the more normal which we got despite the rain.

Since I was on leave and not R&R I did not have a reserved seat returning to Saigon. This meant I could be flexible as long as I didn't go too far – such as spending a month there. Gillian at the R&R center asked if I'd like to go to her parent's rural vacation house the next weekend and I, of course, accepted. In the meantime I bounced around Sydney for a couple of days before following Andy Patten's suggestion and going to RAAF Williamtown. The base was near Newcastle and a short hop on a commuter flight. I walked into the Officer's Club in the afternoon and found a fairly large number of officers present. I was welcomed after mentioning Andy's name and it turned into a long, a very long, social afternoon and evening. I did find out that there was a significant battle raging around Moung Soui but that was not much of a surprise.

I was barely coherent when I got into bed at 0300 the next morning. After a bit over three hours sleep I was awakened by a batman, took a shower, and went to breakfast. I really, truly, felt like hell warmed over and was stunned to see the very same characters of a few hours before sitting there looking chipper and wide-awake. I began to wonder if these guys all had twin brothers, or perhaps interchangeable livers. They did ask me if I knew what tomorrow was and I shook my head, slowly, and said no. "Fourth of July, Yank, gonna have to get you drunk tonight". Groan. I was given an hour long flight in a Winjeel, a tail-dragger trainer, and managed to keep breakfast down. I paced myself as much as possible

CHAPTER SEVEN

and did get to bed earlier than the previous night but I was certainly not fully functional when a Corporal drove me to the outgoing commuter flight the next morning.

The Corporal introduced me to the sole pilot of the Beech 99, declaring that I was a Yank Air Force pilot. The commuter pilot put me in the right cockpit seat and away we went to Sydney. After we leveled off he handed the airplane off to me and went in back to check on something. I was stunned. There I was flying an airplane I had never seen before, one full of passengers, and I was technically not in the best of shape but I managed to maintain heading, altitude, and airspeed while the pilot was gone. It might be something to think about the next time you get on a commuter flight.

Being on leave status meant I had to process through the R&R center every morning that I might depart, and get myself and my luggage on the airport bus. One morning, on the way to the airport, the bus stopped at a stoplight and a Navy enlisted guy opened the door and ran away. Well, I had a seat on the plane.

I arrived back at Tan Son Nhut late in the afternoon of 12 July and found that the next Scatback to Udorn would be in the morning. Having had all the fun I could stand at Camp Alpha I looked up my pilot training classmate, Russ Mullen. Russ was away but I got to use a bunk in his room. I had dinner and a few drinks in the nearby Officer's Club and, unfortunately, had attracted a number of people at my table because of the black flight suit. They, all junior officers, turned out to be on the staff at 7th Air Force. One of them, hesitating a bit, asked if I knew that Ly Lue had been killed that day at Moung Soui. I felt like I'd been hit in the chest with a 2 x 4, lurching forward slightly as tears ran down my face. I didn't have much to say and I think the others were a bit embarrassed in a way. I was anxious to get back to work.

125

'Things at Long Tieng had changed in the sense that there was a greater tenseness in what had always been a tense environment. The NVA had taken Moung Soui, the Neutralists fleeing westward, abandoning a Thai artillery battalion, and leaving the NVA in a position to cut the north/south Route 13 or conduct a difficult 25 mile advance towards Long Tieng, or perhaps both. The death of Ly Lue, shot down by 12.7 mm near Moung Soui, put a cloud over everyone. The weather was gloomy and rainy and working flights, even slow movers, was more difficult and demanding.

In my absence there had also been some personnel changes. Walt Ackerlund had left about the time I went to Australia and was not replaced with a "senior" Raven. On the other hand, we now had an "Air Officer Commanding" (AOC) to advise the Hmong RLAF pilots and, in a sense, to oversee us. The individual was Joe Potter, perfect for the job. He had left the Air Force in 1964 and became a contract CIA T-28 pilot and, when that program was phased out, flew for Air America for four years. Having violated the three strikes and you are out rule – wrecking three airplanes – he had managed to get back into the Air Force. He was canny, a great practical joker, and a good friend until his early death in 1981.

I found that while my somewhat prolonged absence from the battle area was necessary for my own stability, absence from the constant pressure of combat made me about a half a step too slow on my return. This was, I was to find, a common phenomenon and a potentially dangerous one. It took a few days to get back up to speed. Two new Ravens arrived, Smoky Greene and Bob Dunbar, and quickly got to work. A third new Raven arrived and I spent a couple of days checking him out.

The third guy seemed to be somehow not quite up to speed but he was, well, okay. On his third day he went out for his first solo ride, carrying the backseater that had been with me in the U-17 at LS 198 in June. Frank Shaw and I both cautioned him that his O-1 had a leaky carb gasket and he should be on the ground after no more than three hours after takeoff. He acknowledged and away he went. I took off in my O-1 a bit later and headed north, listening to the new guy working a flight. I'd need to talk to him, I thought, since he needed a few tips. I was to learn how fast things can happen in that environment.

In my absence the new guy flew more than three hours, realized that he didn't have enough fuel to get back to 20A and so decided to land at LS 20, Sam Thong, across Skyline ridge from 20A. LS 20 was a busy place and more "civilian" oriented with USAID there and that sort of activity. He was about a quarter-mile on final when the engine quit. He might have made it but he put down full flaps, 60 degrees in an O-1, and went in nose-first. He must have come from the O-2 and had a minimal O-1 checkout since full flaps is not a good idea in the O-1. The backseater apparently was not strapped in so he slammed forward, smashing the new guy into the instrument panel. The new guy had a fractured skull and the magneto switch driven into a kneecap. The backseater was dead.

A HH-53 "Jolly Green" was, as usual, sitting alert at 20A. Doc Quinby convinced them to takeoff and haul him and Frank Shaw over to the crash site which, after their usual procedural delays, they did. They landed near the wreckage and the Doc and Frank went over, assessed things, and Frank started using bolt cutters to cut the new guy out of the wreckage. They asked the Jolly crew for help more than once and were refused since this, apparently, did not fit into their job description. Frank walked the short distance to the Sam Thong ramp and a couple of Air America guys brought over a stretcher. Air America carried the new guy to an Air America Porter which transported the Doc and Frank back to 20A and then hauled the new guy to the Air Force hospital at Udorn. He recovered and spent his Raven days at another site. This, along with another sin soon to come, prompted us to eventually have the Jolly Green crews do their alert time in their HH-53 and not in our house.

Joe Potter felt that the T-28 would make a good and necessary addition to the Raven inventory and proceeded to do the necessary politicking to get that concept implemented. The AIRA office set a rule that those with more time left on their tour would be checked out first. Cavanaugh who was to leave in early October used his usual slick charm and checked out first. I extended my tour until December and got the four hour checkout at Udorn near the end of the month.

In the meantime there were some other interesting and different factors in our, certainly my, operational environment. We seemed to be getting a lot more secondary explosions and fires resulting from strikes. This would appear that the NVA was pushing more supplies forward, or perhaps we were just getting lucky. Another minor factor was the appearance most days of a four-ship of F-105 carrying two Mark 118 3000 pound bombs each. The Thuds had to release both at the same time resulting in four passes total with a very large amount of O-1 window-flexing explosive power. While this may sound neat there was a real question about what to do with this ordnance. We were pretty sure the Air Force was just getting rid of this stuff since the bomb was fairly thinly cased and couldn't penetrate well and, because of its tremendous blast effect, had an 800m safe distance making working it around friendlies improbable.

I thought back to when Scar and I worked the Thud that skipped two 2000 pounders into the NVA armored personnel carrier. That blast effect had killed 21 NVA hiding in a cave about 200m away, with the cave entrance facing away from the blast. Northern Laos was riddled with caves and the enemy used them for storage, troop billeting, and head-

CHAPTER SEVEN

quarters functions. As an example, the main cave at Xieng Khoung had a small hospital, bunks for 700 troops, and extended so far to the north that the Hmong checking it out decided, after walking over a kilometer, that maybe they had better things to do. So, why not start planting those massive explosions at cave mouths? And so I started doing that in a process that lasted for at least ten weeks. There was little or no visible evidence of this practice causing the hoped for results, until long after the fact. Somebody besides the NVA did notice however. Several years later when I worked in the Pentagon a fighter pilot walked past me and murmured, "cave buster".

The T-28 checkout at Udorn took three days and totaled 4 hours of instruction. It was an easy plane to fly, it after all had started life as a trainer. The main issue was not over-priming the big 1425 horsepower radial engine during the somewhat complex start sequence. That would result in an embarrassing stack fire.

`The start process became an almost mechanical over time, but one in which awareness was important. After you are all strapped in and ready to go, turn the tank selector on the left console outboard to the ALL position. Then open the throttle about an inch, move the prop lever to FULL INCREASE, mixture to CUTOFF. Check generator OFF and battery ON. Lean forward and to the right, shoulder straps chaffing, and punch down with your right middle finger on the starter button on the forward right console. The starter cranks the fat three-bladed prop energetically with a grinding whine that goes back to World War II.

Count nine blades jerking past before switching the magnetos to ON and beginning to jab at the PRIME button with an increasing tempo using your right index finger. Not enough and the engine won't have enough fuel to start, too much and a stack fire will blaze into your face across the windscreen. With a coughing judder the engine catches,

MEETING STEVE CANYON

sighs, belches some gray-white smoke, and begins a jerky roar as you get off PRIME while pushing the mixture to RICH, battery OFF, generator ON. Jockey the throttle until the engine evens out. Run the cowl flaps to full open. Turn on the FM, VHF, and UHF radios along with the ADF and TACAN/VOR. See, it's not that complicated.

I suppose the Major instructor who had spent his career in Training Command actually thought I was lying in bed at my hotel at night and reading the dash 1 (aircraft manual) and memorizing emergency procedures. It dawned on me during my last checkout ride, as he had me enter a spin, that he was giving me a check ride. When we sat at his desk at Det 1 after the ride this was confirmed when he started asking me emergency procedures that I was supposed to have memorized. He said, "What do you do if you have an engine failure on takeoff"? He was not amused when I replied, "Where I live, probably die". He said to answer the question and that this wasn't funny. This is where being a Raven was rewarding if a bit improper by conventional norms. I leaned forward and said, "Look Major, I don't care if you sign that Form 8 (check ride certification) or not. In 20 minutes I'm taking off in 566 (a T-28 parked on the ramp) and heading north." He glared and signed the paperwork.

Getting some T-28 into the hands of the Ravens took more than Joe Potter's work. He had the help of some of the Air Commando old heads who worked in the AIRA office. The same team went to work again when Det 1 did indeed supply us with a couple of T-28, but those were not as fully modified as the best they had. This meant we were given B/C models with a "suitcase" .50 caliber machine gun on each wing with a total of 200 rounds. Worse, they had normal parachutes, not the Yankee extraction system that got you out of the airplane near instantaneously. The Yankee (the screwdriver company) system blew a hole in the canopy, the rocket whipped you (not the seat) through the hole, and straps zipped open the chute. The system was certified for 250 feet inverted or 30 feet in a 60 degree bank. One of the Det 1 instructors remarked that we shouldn't have the Yankee-equipped planes since "their job was more dangerous than ours". It kind of makes you wonder. The Air Commando types took care of that issue.

As mentioned previously, we had occasional problems with A-1 attack sorties, which seemed almost counter-intuitive given that it was a slow prop driven aircraft specifically designed for accurate close air support. Some of the A-1 results were so bad we wondered if some of the pilots were part of some sub-set of the anti-war movement. The first flight I worked in my T-28D was an A-1 two-ship. I directed them against a bunch of hootches on the southern edge of the PDJ. As soon as I marked the area a bunch of Pathet Lao ran into the open and started blazing away. How did I know they were PL? Simple, they looked ratty and PL did stupid things like run into the open and shoot ineffectively at armed aircraft. The A-1 did a credible job and as they were completing their last strafe pass I called and said I would put one rocket (WP) in a hootch I identified. I fired at a slant range of about 2000 feet. The rocket went through the door of the hootch and the whole thing exploded. The A-1 lead was astounded. "how much time you got in that '28", he asked. "Coming up on 6 hours" was my smirky reply". It was pure luck.

Flying the T-28D was great fun, acting as your own engine of destruction when needed, which seemed to be all the time. Being a low-wing airplane, it was certainly not ideal for observation purposes but that level of perfection was not always required in our situation. It cruised at about 140 knots indicated with the drag of four rocket pods and had three hours of fuel. In the case of the T-28, three hours meant three hours and you better be on the ground next to a fuel pump. While 140 does not seem to be very fast by aircraft standards, it was as fast as I could stand when it came to flying up creek beds to Long Tieng in bad weather, and we were having lots of marginal weather.

In the meantime the modifications on our existing house were completed and a new house next door was under construction with a target completion date of early October. The modifications to the existing house moved the radio room from what had been a cramped closet to a more open area next to the new "map room" which was really a sort of administrative area. We now also had a more social bar arrangement that was enclosed. All this made for a little more sleeping room but we really needed the new house with the growing numbers of people. One other, rather odd, piece of equipment arrived one morning with a couple of Air Force technicians. It was a secure teletype with which our radio operator could connect directly to Blue Chip in Saigon, or the AIRA office, or who knows who else. Even at that time I thought that this was the big Air Force trying gather us closer into the fold, a thought prompted by a remark by an AIRA type that now we didn't have to rely on CIA communications. Yes, a rather strange thought process. Contrary to what Air Force "historians" may think and later wrote, we did not receive target lists or Air Tasking Orders on that teletype, or through any other communications means.

One evening in the first part of August we were informed by CIA that Vang Pao and his troops would take the Plain of Jars and surrounding areas in an operation named ABOUT FACE. We were to receive up to 100 fighter/attack sorties per day to support this operation and that level of support would continue for the foreseeable future. This was an increase of about 60% over our current sortie level. Mike Byers had arrived to replace Bob Passman so we had six Ravens (although Dan Davis went on a couple of weeks of home leave) that were about to be busy all the time.

I think some of us, including some CIA case officers, had some reservations about this operation that was scheduled to begin on 15 August

CHAPTER SEVEN

1969. One of them was the weather. If it continued as it had for the last couple of months it would be very difficult to support a large ground operation effectively and consistently. The second concern was a basic shift in operational practice on the part of the Hmong. They had been involved in mostly guerilla type warfare for a very long time. Full scale conventional operations, particularly against a well-equipped somewhat conventional army, was something with which the Hmong had little experience. This was a strategy shift from bleeding the NVA, and delaying them, by using guerilla operations supported by heavy air activity, to a much more direct conventional confrontation with even heavier air support. There were only so many Hmong, could they succeed and for how long?

One concern evaporated, literally, on 15 August. The miserable weather in which we had been struggling disappeared overnight and that day was bright with sunshine in a nearly cloudless sky. This sudden, almost miraculous, change gave Vang Pao plenty to smile about since he repeatedly said that the weather would be good, no matter what we farang thought. The man had an impressive ability to see the near future and that apparently included the weather. And so we got to work preparing the way for friendly force advances which came, initially, from the southwestern PDJ area. One of the strikes I worked that day was a good example of the advantage of a combination of experience and a sense of the battlefield.

A communications intercept indicated that there was a NVA communications center and battalion command post somewhere in the west end of Ban Ban valley. There were near-term plans for the friendlies, mostly Lao Special Guerilla Units (SGU), to seize and hold a high point named Phu Na Kok, located on the east side of Route 7 where it exited Ban Ban. Eliminating enemy communications and command elements would be a good start.

MEETING STEVE CANYON

When looking for something like this it is useful to remember that few people like to climb things repeatedly or to be too far from water. Those two factors alone cut down the search area quite a bit. In the southwest corner of the valley there were plenty of trees and vegetation and a good-sized stream winding its way westward.

As I circled, not something you wanted to do much in Ban Ban, there was a flash of reflection off a blade antenna that had been attached to the top of a tree. The NVA were not going to park themselves and their radios next to an antenna, no matter how difficult it was to identify. I looked a reasonable distance south, closer to the stream, and mentally outlined an area that probably contained the target. VEGAS, three F-4D, saturated an 800 meter circle with 9 cans of CBU 24 and 36 Mark 82 in a few minutes. I could see numerous NVA running through some of the few clearings in the trees, and five that would run no more.

A couple of days later came another "special mission" of the same type as before – a meeting between a political commissar from Hanoi and a regimental commander and his staff. Since I was flying a T-28 and had lots of WP rockets (28), I marked a box around where the meeting was and had AGILE, three F-4, "fill the box". An interesting development was that the NVA accused the Pathet Lao of talking too much and that was how the Americans found out the where and when of the meeting. The CIA, somehow, managed to fan the flames and there was actually a shoot-out between some PL and NVA with casualties on both sides. The odd thing about this was that the NVA routinely listened to our uncoded tactical communications and couldn't, or wouldn't, quite make the mental leap that their coded communications had been breached.

Before I took off in the T-28 for that special mission, Dan Davis appeared on the ramp having returned from home leave and a check out in the T-28. He wanted to fly the T-28 I had been flying but I declined

CHAPTER SEVEN

since I'd have to move my stuff to an O-1. There was always another day so Dan took off in an O-1 to get back in the game. Unfortunately, like all of us returning from a longish leave, he was a little slow in circumstances that were ever-demanding and increasingly hectic in every regard.

Dan was working a four-ship of F-105 near the west end of Ban Ban when one of the Thuds hit Dan's O-1 in a mid-air collision. The potential for such accidents was with us during every strike but that didn't make it any easier to accept. The Thud pilot thought he had been hit by anti-aircraft fire and recovered at Udorn. The rest of the flight returned to their base, having lost contact with the Raven. The Thud at Udorn, I was told later, had some fabric stuck in the paint on the bottom side of his nose. The only fabric in an O-1 are the seat cushions. Dan's remains were recovered in 1995.

Andy Patten flew up and spent the evening talking to us about this sort of thing, and assuring me that it wasn't my fault. Larry the radio operator had tuned in the Voice of America on his HF set and it was very eerie that evening to hear a scratchy, hissing rendition of "Yankee Doodle Dandy" followed by a deep voice announcing that "... this ... is the ... Voice of America ...".

The next day General Vang Pao once again demonstrated his ability to see the near future. He had been flown to Vientiane by Air America to attend a conference about the current operation. The Air America Huey remained at Wattay airport, along with others, until Vang Pao returned. As events were told to us later, he got into the Huey and sat down, looked around and shook his head, stood up and left the Huey saying something like "... not this airplane today ..." and proceeded to get in another Huey which took off for Long Tieng. The original Huey cranked up and also took off proceeding in the same direction. Approximately a half hour after takeoff the helicopter exploded. It appeared

135

that someone had dropped a taped grenade in the gas tank, a very old and very lethal trick.

We continued to hit supply dumps, troop concentrations, and fortified positions with often fairly dramatic results. The NVA were getting hammered and the friendlies were advancing where they found enemy weakness, a condition that was becoming more common. In addition to close support in TIC situations, we continued our long-time practice of following up on intelligence and recon team reporting in locating and striking supplies and supply routes to the North Vietnamese border and, occasionally, beyond. The "beyond" part involved taking a T-28 five to ten miles into North Vietnam and attacking supplies and troops. This was certainly contrary to US policy and direction but we were involved in fighting a major battle and were little impressed with artificial restrictions. The North Vietnamese, by the way, never complained about our intrusions or "violations" of US policy direction. They knew the price of the game.

Much has been written over the years about sensors dropped by the Air Force that relayed information, through relay aircraft, to a central processing facility at Nakhon Phanom. This program, referred to as Igloo White, was directed towards interdicting the supply flow of North Vietnamese troops and supplies southward along the Ho Chi Minh trail.

The Air Force, over CIA opposition, decided to make sensor drops in Northern Laos for the same purpose. I think the CIA opposition was based largely on the issue of turf, as was the Air Force position. CIA relied, particularly at night, on road watch teams that were able to communicate with A-1 aircraft via VHF radio and successfully control air strikes on enemy forces traveling along "lines of communication" (LOC). This practice worked fairly well and the CIA wanted to continue to maintain fairly close control over where and how airpower was used

CHAPTER SEVEN

in what was, after all, their operation. There were additional related factors involving protection of friendly teams and villages, and other more opaque reasons. The Air Force wanted to go the sensor route and did.

Road watch teams could not communicate with fast-movers nor would their control be effective given the speeds involved. The Air Force wanted to get into the interdiction business, on a more informed basis, to demonstrate what they believed was a superior capability that would achieve superior results. Unsaid, of course, was that the Air Force wanted to not only keep their hand in the game but to expand its scope. The increased use of fast Fac , operating on Air Force generated "intelligence", was one way to do this, adding sensor data to the pot was another way. The "History of the War in Northern Laos" goes so far as to state that only the Air Force, operating on their own, was capable of conducting useful interdiction because the area in question was "too hot for props". Well, one wonders if this was written under duress.

On August 21st, following procedures outlined to us, I worked two sensor drop missions. My job was to mark the beginning of their drop pattern, something done at a very low altitude. That mark was merely to confirm that they had not made some gross error with the LORAN system on their F-4. The first drop was in Ban Ban valley on Route 61 a bit north of where it intersects with Route 7. Heeding their accuracy requirement I took my O-1 down to a couple of hundred feet to fire a rocket. I was a bit dismayed to hear one of the F-4 announce that I was 50 feet long. They were gone in seconds but I spent what seemed a very long time climbing out of that death trap valley. LORAN, about which I knew nothing, certainly seemed accurate. Their drop ran diagonally across Route 61 which I thought was an invitation for the NVA to look for something since this whole show would have looked pretty odd to

MEETING STEVE CANYON

them. Another flight dropped farther up Route 61 at a very narrow place with steep drop-offs on both sides. We never heard, of course, if they got useful information out of this exercise.

That had been an exhausting day, In addition to the sensor drops I had worked 26 sorties in 12 air strikes. That level of activity, requiring constant thinking and maneuvering, makes one bone-tired and brain weary by the time the sun went down. Fortunately, we were having spots of bad weather which let the grinding fatigue set in a bit more slowly. One bright spot, soon to arrive, was the wedding of Vang Pao's oldest son. It would be a traditional ceremony on the 26th followed by a somewhat lavish reception which most of the farang would attend. Vang Pao, by the way, had six wives (simultaneously) and 26 children so, theoretically, there would be a lot of weddings.

The day had been relatively light for me but a giant party sounded like a great idea. The farang gathered in a sort of reception area with dirt floors and included almost all the Raven personnel, two Army guys who had been at Moung Soui, Air America and Continental types, and some Thai Special Operations men. Colonel Tyrell, the Air Attache, visited briefly and left before sundown so he could get back to Vientiane before the sun went down. He exchanged the appropriate words with Vang Pao and a few others but had little to say to us. I would see him one more time before I departed. In any event, we all ate exotic snacks and shots of White Horse Scotch served on silver platters carried by young Hmong girls. I think the only thing that kept most of us going was the high adrenaline rate we experienced on a routine basis. The tallest guy in the crowd was a legendary Continental pilot, Al Adolph. When Al left I was the tallest guy in the area, six foot four, and that is when the trouble started.

A Thai, they were all associated with Thai Special Operations, approached me and looked up at me with his deep brown eyes. He,

CHAPTER SEVEN

like most Thais, was slender and fairly small. "I am Captain Peng", he said, "I don't like Americans and I am going to kill you". I laughed at what seemed to be a silly joke. Peng did not smile and started rummaging in a pocket in his trousers.

I looked down towards the dirt floor where Frank Shaw, one of our well-regarded maintenance guys, was sitting. Frank had a serious look on his face when he shook his head back and forth. This definitely meant that Peng was trouble. Peng extracted a pocket knife from his trousers and started fumbling with one of the blades. I laughed again because it looked a lot like a Boy Scout pocket knife I had when I was a kid. He unfolded a curved blade that, I think, was supposed to be used for punching holes in leather or something. I stopped laughing when I saw that it had been turned on a grinding wheel so that it was razor sharp along the edges and at the point. Before I could say anything else Peng's right hand lunged at my neck and I could feel him starting to cut as blood spurted down my shirt and speckled on him. I may have been pretty drunk but I was still very fast as my right hand grabbed his small right wrist and crushed it, pulling it away and forcing him down. I snatched the knife away and unfolded the remaining blades, snapping them off the handle one by one, stepping on them and jerking.

I aimed myself for the screen door and started walking the couple of hundred yards to our house, my right hand resting on where the blood seemed to be leaking. Instead of going into our house I decided that maybe giving a CIA guy a tip about Peng might be a good idea. I opened a door to a room at the CIA house where I knew there would be guys playing poker. Facing the door was Burr Smith, one hand raised about to put some chips on the table. The front of my shirt was pretty well covered with blood and that got his attention.

"What the hell happened to you", he said, his hand suspended in mid-air. "Captain Peng said he doesn't like Americans so maybe you should watch out", I said, focused on Burr. To my right there was a voice and I turned to see Colonel Dhep, Deputy for Thai Special Operations at the time. "If Captain Peng tried to kill you tonight, he will try to kill me tomorrow", he said in a firm but unemotional voice. I nodded and left, going to our house to see Doc Quinby, knowing that Peng was in real trouble.

Grif cleaned off the wound area, a relatively small puncture on the left side of my larynx with a cut heading towards a major artery. When Grif was done he put a band aid on the cut and said I was good to go. I was both grateful and a bit disappointed. Enough blood to soak a shirt and all I got is a band aid.

Morning came early and busy as it always was but I did see a sullen, escorted, Captain Peng getting into an unmarked Thai aircraft that was parked on the ramp. When I later asked what had happened to Captain Peng, a knowledgeable CIA officer merely said that he had been "sent back to Thailand in disgrace". On the other hand, Colonel Dhep had a reputation for disposing of his problems in another fashion. The Thai aircraft was undoubtedly in Thai airspace when Peng got "airmailed", as the phrase went.

CHAPTER EIGHT

September was a dynamic month that saw great military successes on the ground, evidence of evolving challenges in that arena, a complex special mission, and some fairly incredible interactions that were dismaying to the Ravens and, undoubtedly, to others.

Elements of the NVA 312th Division in the southwestern Plain of Jars area began withdrawing eastward due to continuing pressure from Hmong forces, intense and continuing close air support strikes by both the USAF and RLAF, and significant supply interdiction along established roads and newly established supply trails. Some of that road interdiction was accomplished by the fast FAC programs but most was done by Ravens, especially the trail networks of which we were made aware on a continuing basis. Additionally, CIA-led attacks on an outpost, Phou Na Kok, at the west end of Ban Ban Valley had begun. Phou Na Kok was on the east side of Route 7 where it exited Ban Ban to the west. LS-32 was a few miles to the north on the other side of the road.

The close air support in the southwest PDJ area had consisted of constant hammering of the NVA through the hills and jungle to the southwest. It continued once the NVA were pushed onto the PDJ but did not last long since there were few places they could hide and still provide effective resistance. Additionally, they were running low on supplies and troops.

My most vivid memory of this phase was strafing NVA positions on the PDJ with the friendlies no more than 10 meters away. I was low enough in the T-28 to barely clear the faces I could see very well. As the NVA faded eastward a forward supply auxiliary air strip was set up in that corner of the PDJ so that Air America and Continental could provide rapid supply and reinforcement to the friendlies. It was also a place where we could refuel and rearm our O-1 aircraft, significantly cutting our turnaround time. One major problem developed at that aux field and it had to do with food.

There were large numbers of water buffalo on the PDJ. There were also water buffalo at Long Tieng and other areas where the Hmong were concentrated but those buffalo were essential for farming. The PDJ buffalo represented a meat supply. That would have been alright had the buffalo been processed through some magically appearing slaughter house facility, if such a thing existed. Since such a thing did not exist the Hmong would simply shoot a buffalo and carve off what they wanted at the moment and leave the rest to rot. If the wind was blowing the wrong way, refueling and rearming got to be a more and more dismaying process since a few dozen rotting buffalo carcasses can supply a very strong stench to an area.

I did land there one day carrying a rare, for me, backseater who volunteered to run off and get us some lunch. He came back with a piece of buffalo that had maggots crawling out of it, sort of ending any desire I had for lunch. Maggots, I was told in survival school, are very high in protein and perfectly good to eat. Perhaps it was the presentation. Soon the aux field was surrounded with dead buffalo and the smell was overwhelmingly awful. Even the Air America Filipino crew chiefs had had enough so they pumped aviation fuel on the carcasses and burned them one day. The next two forward aux fields did not have a repeat of this situation, lessons having been learned.

CHAPTER EIGHT

Our experiences in this part of ABOUT FACE made us realize that the fighter pilots were so used to working random patterns that the concept of a racetrack for close air support was something that they had forgotten. Mike Cavanaugh and I went to Udorn, turning in some planes for maintenance, and gave a couple of impromptu presentations at a fighter squadron concerning why we sometimes needed a fighter racetrack and why. It did smooth things out a bit, but the use of that pattern remained very limited due to the ground fire situation.

One aspect of the ground fire environment was that the friendlies were capturing an increasing number of 37mm anti-aircraft guns, all of which had flowed through the USSR as part of World War II lend-lease, or had been manufactured there. The number of guns needed or wanted for display purposes was limited so Burr Smith enthusiastically, as with everything else he did, began the job of blowing up captured guns.

It was a learning experience for Burr and a source of some humor for the rest of us. His initial approach to the job was to place a large charge of C-4 plastic explosive on a gun and get a considerable distance away before he detonated the C-4. The first problem was the distance equaled delay and delay could, and almost did, have Hmong wandering into the soon-to-be-explosion area. The second problem was he was using way too much C-4. His first gun was nearly vaporized, hurling shredded parts for way too far. He learned from experience quickly and soon got it down to a very modest whump that destroyed the gun's functionality without causing a steel rain.

One of the stranger airstrikes I ever worked took place the day after I got back from my lecture trip to Udorn. I only worked that afternoon in my T-28 but that included seven airstrikes, the last one providing the entertainment. I got a call from remote site very close to the North Vietnamese border near the "Fish's Mouth", which is what the border looked

MEETING STEVE CANYON

like on a map.. The site was being mortared and when I arrived it was very easy to see the tube flash from two mortars as they continued firing. The beginning of darkness as the sun was setting made observation easier in this case. I decided to do the night A-1 and A-26 guys a favor and have them take out the mortars and NVA troops. ZORRO 51 and 52, the A-1, and NIMROD 30, a solo A-26, normally did night work in Barrel Roll. This was not at all fun given the terrain, marginal navigation aids in some areas, and the ease with which disorientation could occur. It was past official sunset so it was legally a "night mission".

I marked the mortar location and told ZORRO to spread his ordnance around. Pass after pass dumped several tons of napalm, bombs, and rockets on the mortar positions. The site radio operator had never seen anything like this and was breathing hard in my ear. Then NIMROD dumped something like six cans of nape and six 500 pounders making the area probably two feet deep in nape and shredded trees. When they were done I fired off my remaining WP rockets and then strafed any possible hiding places. When I pulled off and headed home for an uninviting night landing on our unlit runway, the radio operator gave me a very subdued "tank you, Raben".

Our cook, SSGT Manual "Espi" Espinosa, had the reached the end of his time in Southeast Asia and left our old teak house for greener pastures. We all hoped that he, for the sake of his future customers, got over his fixation with pork. We waited a bit for Espi's replacement and found that the AIRA office had no intention of replacing him or asking anyone else for a replacement. This meant that one of us had to both arrange for supplies and do the cooking. Aside from the fact that none of us knew much about cooking, there was the reality that we were all working a tremendous amount and didn't have the time to take on a cooking job. The maintenance guys were working at maximum capacity, to the extent

CHAPTER EIGHT

that one would sometimes find them at dawn dozing under an airplane. Ravens were flying 150 to 200 hours a month, far more than was "legal", in an extremely hostile environment. A little more bitterness about AIRA crept into our minds.

The effort to take Phu Na Kok continued with numerous ground assaults and was clearly going to succeed at some point soon. The NVA were in fortified positions in a roughly circular compound and when I started working an F-4 four-ship a sort of miracle happened. The F-4 were carrying four Mark 84 2000 pounders each, not a usual load. I briefed them and marked the target, cautioning them that friendlies were downslope to the north. Lead rolled in and I, directly behind him, could see that he was pointed about 15 degrees off heading and would miss the whole compound and hit who-knew-what. As my thumb tightened on the mike switch to tell him to go through dry, he pulled left, towards the compound, pulled up releasing two of the bombs which arced very high heading...somewhere. I radioed the friendlies to get down. This looked like it would be Duc Lap plantation repeated. I was fairly close when the two bombs came whistling down and impacted in the middle of the compound. I could see the concussion collapsing a tunnel network the NVA had built (they did love tunnels). I asked lead if he thought he could repeat that maneuver. His reply was, "Hell, no". We proceeded to pound the compound which was soon overrun by the friendlies and then held for months while repelling repeated NVA ground assaults.

Mike Byers had an unusual conversation on the ramp one morning with Father Luke Bouchard, a Catholic priest and missionary. Father Bouchard had been on a Communist kill list for years but his scattered flocks made his travels safe, perhaps with some additional help. Luke approached Mike and told him that one of his long-ago parishioners in the Sam Nuea area had told him that their former church had become an ammunition dump and that Mike was free to take it out. Mike replied that the information was nice but he didn't know where Luke's former church was located. Luke looked around and then reached under his blue cotton work shirt, pulled out a 1:50000 map, and pointed to the location. Mike said it made a large explosion.

The NVA made it a practice to store fuel and ammunition in religious facilities based on the assumption, I am sure, that Americans wouldn't bomb a church so to speak. Father Bouchard's efforts had produced a few "churches" but there were plenty of Buddhist temples, called a wat, scattered around, particularly in the PDJ area. The temple would be situated inside a circular ring of trees with the ground around the temple cleared of vegetation. From the air it looked like a bulls-eye, which was a handy reference. Buddhist monks today complain about damaged or destroyed temples but they were supply dumps then and their predecessors had no say in the matter.

Luke Bouchard spent 19 years in Laos and, for the most part, hiked on trails to get from one place to another. If you have people like that available to you, and you ask questions, you do learn a lot about the local society and events. Air America was not supposed to fly Luke around but they did from time to time. Luke was hiking from Long Tieng to LS 15, a ten minute flight or two days of walking, in what became a hellacious rainstorm that wouldn't go away. He heard the sound of a Huey almost overhead so he whipped out the VHF handset someone had given him. "Helicopter near site fifteen this is Father Bouchard, you are overhead can you pick me up?", he said in a strained voice as the rain poured down. The Huey pilot replied, "How do I know this is Father Bouchard? If you are really Father Bouchard, make a sign". A bewildered Bouchard replied, "Make a sign? What do you want me to do?". "I want you", the Huey pilot replied, "to make it stop raining". He got picked up. It didn't stop raining.

CHAPTER EIGHT

One evening, before mid-September, at a post-VP dinner meeting, the CIA base chief, Tom, talked to me alone about some imagery they had received from the Air Force. He pushed a print across the table to me, the imagery dated in June almost 90 days before. The imagery was from an RF-4 mission flown out of Udorn and showed signals on the ground that had been composed of large scale soil mounds built between a mountain rice paddy area and a large stream that ran south from Sam Nuea in stair-step like bends. The mounds were big enough that any ground observers not involved in the effort would simply see them as some kind of flood control effort, or some such. The mounds were very clear in spelling out "SOS" but the last "S" was backwards. These letters, on the east side of the stream, were tucked next to a perfect outline of an F-105 and an arrow pointing northwest across the stream to a village a few hundred meters away and somewhat elevated above the stream. It was obviously a signal from US prisoners-of-war. "We got this this morning," he said, "and at Udorn yesterday ... the Air Force, as you can see from the print, took this in June and couldn't figure out to do with it so they finally handed it off to us."

He knew what I was thinking, undoubtedly thoughts that he had before our meeting. The Air Force acquired imagery that potentially identified a location for USAF prisoners, a rare commodity in Laos, and then kicked it around, undoubtedly in Saigon, for three months before throwing up their hands. The distance, by the way, from where the film was originally processed and interpreted to the CIA facility at Udorn was about one mile. That was pretty disgusting performance, at a minimum. "What do you want me to do", I said.

"I would like you to troll the area in a T-28 and see what you think, see if it's a flak trap" he paused and watched me arch my eyebrows since we both knew that Sam Nuea was a dangerous place. "We have good information that the 57mm gun they have there is inop", he said, continuing, "we recently extracted a team from the area . . . they got into a shoot-out in the village the arrow points at". I looked at the picture for another minute. "Okay, I'll try it in the morning and we'll see what happens . . . and I hope you're right about that 57". A 57 mm would shred a T-28 or most other aircraft with a near, explosive, miss.

I went back to our bar and had some Johnnie Walker Black and thought about what was probably happening to the Americans who might be there and what tomorrow might bring. Looking around our bar, watching some of the other Ravens and maintenance guys, I sensed how the grinding pressure and fatigue was affecting us. We were quieter, perhaps more introspective, perhaps withdrawing a bit into a protective cocoon from which we ventured every morning and slogged through another relentless day. There were other people flying other airplanes in other places who thought they were really close to the edge of the abyss. We, and Air America, and Continental, and the CIA could probably tell them about a different world. Yet, we had volunteered to do what we were doing, for a variety of reasons that differed for each of us. One common reason, perhaps, was to discover what our own limits were and what it took to reach those limits. In the air we were alone, and perhaps that was also true on the ground.

The weather in the morning was barely workable and I had no idea what it would be like in the Sam Nuea area. I had decided to play the role of a defecting Lao pilot so I had maintenance remove the rocket pods from the T-28, they being a signature item for a Raven. I also wore my flight helmet, which I rarely did, so that my face would be partially disguised. I intended to get that low if necessary. I took off and headed north, gray scud arcing up to layers of wet cloud darkening the mixed green of the jungle below. I kept Route 61 in sight as it slanted northeast

CHAPTER EIGHT

towards Sam Nuea. The weather kept me fairly low during this process but I stayed as far from the probably defended road as possible. The weather lightened up a bit as I got closer to Sam Nuea giving me good visibility under what was about a thousand foot ceiling. As I approached the small town that was the Communist capitol of Laos I slowed the T-28 down to about 110 KIAS, dropped half flaps, and opened the canopy about a foot.

The SOS signal was there as I passed, heading for the town a couple of miles away where I would find out if this was a flak trap. The Sam Nuea airstrip was about 3000 feet of grassy dirt, obviously not heavily used, and on the south side of the town. I angled over the strip and around the town, directly over the location of the 57mm gun, and then headed south again, rocking my wings slightly and trying to look lost as I observed what I could. There were occasional bomb craters scattered about, the standing water in them bleached an odd green from explosive chemicals. I was at an altitude between fifty and a hundred feet during most of this. Making another turn around the SOS symbol I looked at it closely and at the village across the stream, but there wasn't much to see. One more trip around the town, I headed south and climbed through the clouds to a reasonable altitude and headed home.

When I arrived back at Long Tieng I asked maintenance to reload the rocket pods since I had work to do. My visit to the base chief was brief and to the point. He said that they would reinsert the team in a few days and he would let me know. I nodded and went back to another day of work which involved attacking the remnants of the 312th Division that were lightly impeding the rapid advance of the friendlies towards the central PDJ. Simultaneously, we were steadily hitting pre-positioned supplies intended for the incoming NVA 316th Division which was inbound to relieve the much battered 312th Division.

Related to this were 26 USAF crash sites in the PDJ area, sites now or soon to be under friendly control. Doc Quinby suggested that he could visit those sites and, if possible, recover bodies or at least survey the situation. Air America was too strapped to provide a helicopter for such an operation so we used the teletype to contact Blue Chip to see if they would provide a couple of HH-3 for such an effort. We indicated that we would also provide a security team. We know the HH-3 squadron in Thailand was not overworked. We received a reply fairly quickly from Blue Chip that said "... it is not worth the effort...". That stunning reply was not exactly a morale booster.

We were able to arrange for Grif and a security team to use an Air America Huey for a morning to visit two crash sites. He recovered the body of an A-1 pilot from one site. At the second site he found things a bit more complicated. In March 1969 an F-105 pulled out of a dive too low and was waddling across the PDJ, gradually recovering from a stall condition. He would have made it but clipped the top of one of the low hills on the Plain. The F-105 exploded. Grif found the pilot's canvas jungle boots, singed and side by side, the laces removed, and a puncture through the canvas from a compound ankle fracture. The NVA would remove boots to keep Americans from running away, and remove the laces to use for tying arms behind the prisoner. There was also a singed G-suit wrapped around the boots. It appeared that the pilot had been taken prisoner, although he must have been badly injured which did not bode well for his survival. We once again messaged Blue Chip with this evidence and again asked for HH-3 support. We got the same answer. It did make one wonder.

A few days later Tom, the CIA base chief, informed Joe Potter and me that the recon team would be inserted the next day to check the potential POW site. An Air America Huey, escorted by two A-1, would insert

CHAPTER EIGHT

the four man team some 10 kilometers south of the target area. They would take about ten days to slowly, quietly, and carefully move through the dense concentrations of hostile forces to reach positions from which they could fully observe the situation at the SOS site and at the village across the stream. Joe, who was not supposed to fly except under very special circumstances, decided that we would escort the escorts. That, he said, was just to ensure that they did their job correctly. While I knew the real reason was he wanted to go flying, his excuse was far too valid given our recent experiences with A-1 pilots.

The next morning the weather was much the same as it had been on my previous visit to the Sam Nuea area. After take-off I got a short lecture from Joe about what a tactical formation was supposed be since I had no clue in that regard. We eventually linked up with the A-1 flight and Air America Huey, covering the Huey as it proceeded to the drop-off point about 10 kilometers from the target area. After about 50 minutes the Huey dropped off the team as the A-1 circled, Joe and I above them. I would make my presence known to the team, as they neared the target area more than a week later. This was not a simple business.

During the entire ABOUT FACE operation CIA nightly messaged the Air Force, CIA, the US embassy in Laos, and who knew who else, on the locations of the main friendly units and the orientation of "no-bomb" lines. We repeated the no-bomb line content to 7th Air Force through our teletype. The friendlies continued their push, moving quickly along the southern PDJ, moving eastward along the central PDJ, making introductory moves from the northwest, and consolidating the area around Phu Na Kok. The first aux strip gave way to a second one a bit closer to the "Xieng Khoung airfield" in the central PDJ. The new aux field had no dead buffalo but there were quite a few trucks riddled by CBU pellets. The Hmong had also captured a number of PT-76 tanks, with more to come, and began to use them in combat to a limited extent – not something I would want to do given the fragility of the PT-76. In addition to other strike activity, we continued to watch the supply build-up along intended routes for the incoming NVA division.

One morning about this time we got some stunning news. The friendlies had taken a large hill near Route 4 on the PDJ during the night, well behind the no-bomb line. The friendlies had set up large identifier letters and a helicopter pad for Air America, a commonly seen phenomena during this and other operations. The weather was a medium overcast with occasional showers but all of this was perfectly visible. A Tiger fast FAC had unilaterally attacked the site, killing 19 friendlies in the process. He had not only violated 7th Air Force directives, he had violated basic common sense norms.

Within a day we learned of another similar error, at least we thought it was an error, in which a village was attacked, again by a Tiger fast FAC running an airstrike, and about 250 friendlies were killed. This was the third attack on friendly forces/population and about 300 had been killed in a couple of weeks. While this was pretty incredible, what really happened was far worse.

I recently learned that 7th Air Force had put that village on a target list which meant it was fair game for any fast FAC or independent USAF directed airstrike (we did not receive target lists from 7th Air Force, but would have reviewed them for legitimacy had we received them). Other villages were also put on a target list. The basis for this was 7th Air Force "intelligence analysis" mostly or wholly relying on imagery interpretation. The fast FAC also had their own imagery interpreters at their respective bases. Paramount among the many problems with this was that the imagery interpreters, by and large, had very limited experience in Southeast Asia, which has different ground signatures for different

CHAPTER EIGHT

reasons in different areas. They also had little or no access to other timely military intelligence sources, such as communications intercepts, which could help confirm imagery "analysis". There was no attempt by the Air Force to contact the US Embassy in Vientiane or the CIA to confirm any of their judgments. The Air Force simply bombed what they thought was enemy-associated, reaching that conclusion based on utter lack of knowledge of an area and an unwillingness to confirm their judgments with people who were both there and were experts. We will never know how many friendlies were killed by this kind of thinking.

Dismayed as we all were by these sorts of events, at the time we put it down to fast FAC ignorance and egotistical outlooks which were prevalent enough. Only in later years did we, or some of us, associate effects with a larger structural cause. It is, after all, not much of a surprise that an organization that bombs Montagnard footpaths would also bomb Hmong villages. The costs, of course, were significantly different. In the meantime, we had to move on with the many tasks at hand. One thing that did change fairly quickly was that the "no bomb line" approach was changed to "Raven boxes". These were fairly large geographical areas in which only Ravens could work air strikes. It really irritated the big Air Force but the Ambassador won.

We were working 80 to 100 sorties per day of fighters in weather that varied from perfect to extremely marginal. The results seemed to be getting more dramatic in terms of fires, explosions, and enemy troop formations destroyed. The ground fire was also increasing in intensity in the areas held by the NVA, pockets of which would remain active behind friendly lines for quite a while.

On a clear and sunny day I took my T-28 to the Sam Nuea area to check on the team that had been inserted. They carried a small HF radio for long distance communication and a VHF for talking to

MEETING STEVE CANYON

aircraft. They, of course, would hear my engine noise somewhere in the area and would contact me if they desired. As I approached Sam Nuea from the west I was startled to see a solitary F-4 rolling in on repeated passes firing single WP rockets into the shallow ravine area south of Sam Nuea about where the SOS marker was located. I called Cricket, got the UHF frequency (fast-movers did not carry VHF) for a TIGER fast FAC, and called asking him what he was doing. His reply was, "Hey, didn't you know, there might be US POW up here". I was stunned beyond disbelief. This idiot was calling attention, with his rocket firing, to an area that had not previously drawn the attention of the NVA/PL. Now he had further focused their attention with his radio transmission which he apparently did not realize was monitored by the NVA. Additionally, of course, he could have hit POW or the approaching team with his rocket fire. I did not reply and left the area, smoldering with anger.

The team was successfully extracted about ten days later. They had arrived in the target area a couple days after the rocket incident and did spend several days in the immediate vicinity of the SOS and the village across the stream. They observed no Americans but they see a few Thai POW. CIA cancelled further operations there since the area was now compromised by the TIGER antics. There is no way of knowing what happened after the Tiger's aerial and talking demonstration but it is highly likely that the NVA/PL, tying a few strings together, started looking around for reasons why someone would think there were "American POW up here". If they did figure it out, the outcome would be extremely unpleasant and terminal for those on the ground. We and/or the CIA had notified the Air Force of the operation for cautionary purposes as was normal and necessary. Incidents were beginning to make us wonder about the wisdom of that procedure. I learned a couple of years ago

CHAPTER EIGHT

that the Tiger pilot was the head of the Tiger FAC program at the time. Sometimes it is useful to give your ego a rest.

Somebody at Udorn came up with an interesting idea sparked, I think, by Laredo observation of what happened every day after the bombing was over, usually about 1730 to 1800. All would be quiet and the bad guys knew it would be mostly that way until tomorrow. What was observed was the smoke from many cooking fires that came from many locations about 20 minutes after the last fighter departed the scene. The Udorn-based squadron selected an area about 3 by 2 miles just northwest of the airfield we were about to occupy. After checking with and getting our okay they went ahead with what they named SNARE DRUM. A number of us, staying well away from dozens of cooking fires, watched as a sixteen ship F-4 formation from the 555th Tactical Fighter Squadron flew to the selected target area at ten thousand feet and dumped 96 cans of radar-fused CBU 24. It was absolutely awesome to see 64000 or so bomblets explode almost simultaneously.

It must have been equally awesome to the NVA since they moved out of that area and went east of Khang Khai. In radio intercepts we read that they considered SNARE DRUM to be "unfair", an attitude which caused a few smiles. They got hit with another SNARE DRUM and that was the last of that technique.

The sweep across the PDJ area permitted us to start using what was known as the Xieng Khong airfield located in about the middle of the PDJ, edged towards the northwest. It was a pierced steel planking (PSP) airfield that had been around since the time of the French Indochina war and before. The wreckage of several abandoned DC-4 transports and other aircraft lined part of the south side of the strip. Hmong troops had secured the site for at least several days before for the necessary support

MEETING STEVE CANYON

moves were made to shift operations there. During this brief period there was one small incident that was funny, and a little not funny.

The USAF Wing Commander of the 56th Special Operations Wing (SOW) at Nakhon Phanom had directed his A-1 pilots not to operate below 3500 feet AGL to prevent them from taking ground fire hits. This was, we were told, not out of some compassion for his pilots but rather his perception that his aircraft taking hits would cloud his chances for promotion to Brigadier General. Unfortunately, dropping ordnance from an A-1 at 3500 feet tended to be pretty inaccurate, particularly unfinned napalm which headed for the next county. Most of the 56th pilots ignored this directive unless they felt they were being observed. One A-1 pilot lost engine oil pressure and landed at the as-yet unoccupied Xieng Khoung airfield. The squad-leader level Hmong troops in the area immediately tied white rags around their left bicep, a recognition signal, as the pilot hesitantly got out of the cockpit and slid off the oil covered wing to the ground, wondering what good his issue .38 would do with what he believed were enemy troops. Fortunately, their US weapons and non-menacing behavior convinced him that all was well.

Air America flew him back to 20A where it turned out that he and Joe Potter were friends from the past. Joe assured him that the A-1 would get lifted out to 20A, be repaired as necessary, and any evidence of battle damage erased. The guy was terribly relieved. We kind of wondered why he didn't know about the white rag recognition signal but didn't press the issue. Either he wasn't told or he didn't listen.

Each of us would go to Vientiane once in a while, sometimes just to take an overnight break. Late one afternoon Joe Potter, who was visiting AIRA for some reason, and I went into an upscale restaurant and bar where Joe, having lived there for years, knew the maitre'd. He was a former French soldier who had been in what was known as the GCMA,

CHAPTER EIGHT

an equivalent of Special Forces, from which he had eventually deserted. After the three of us had a drink Joe and I left the place. When we got outside Joe asked if I noticed anything different about the French guy. I replied that he had hard eyes. "You are getting smarter, kid", replied Joe, informing me that "Jean" was better known as "Jean le Baptiste".

During the French Indochina War he was known as a "knife man" who would slip into Viet Minh troop encampments and cut every other throat, a true psychological burden for the survivors. He, Joe said, still carried a throwing knife held in a thin scabbard just below his neck on his back, just like Hollywood stuff. Joe assured me that in about one second Jean could grab the knife, throw it 25 feet, and stick it through the Ace of Spades symbol on a playing card. I didn't want to find out.

In the nightly dinners at Vang Pao's the deputy CIA base chief would speak to VP in French for sometimes extended periods. I had taken three years of French language in high school but was, like most Americans with that experience, almost completely inept. However, I did find that listening to their conversation for many nights awakened my failed learning experience and I could follow the drift of their dialogue. I discovered that there is a very positive benefit to having some basic language skills, very basic in my case.

Another Raven and I were at the famous "Rendezvous des Amis" in Vientiane one night, talking and having a couple of beers. Lulu, the owner and Madame, was on vacation in France leaving her Lao assistant Madame in charge. The assistant Madame was sitting at a nearby table with two Lao Army officers and they were speaking French which I was following loosely. The important gist of what they said was along the lines of, "... all these terrible things in Laos are because of the farang. If we got rid of the farang we wouldn't have all these problems (fairly true) so, let start by killing those two over there...". Over there being the two of us. I told the other Raven that we were leaving now. He protested that he hadn't finished his beer, but we left anyway. The two Lao Army officers looked very startled.

One of the Hmong T-28 pilots got shot down near Moung Soui one afternoon. He successfully extracted from his airplane but was in an area filled with Vietnamese troops. Bob Dunbar was on the scene almost immediately and tracked the Hmong at very low altitude, calling in periodic strikes to drive off the NVA who seemed determined to capture the Hmong rather than kill him. The hills in that area are fairly modest in height which makes the multiple hits Bob took even more remarkable. Almost all of the hits he took were small arms fire that came from above. One A-1 pilot, his wingman having returned to NKP with engine problems, was delivering sustained firepower at very minimal altitudes. He obviously didn't care about the rules of his Wing Commander. It turned out that the pilot was already on the Colonel promotion list, another reason not to care.

Two Jolly Greens, USAF HH-53 heavy lift rescue helicopters had been on alert at Long Tieng, finally arrived and attempted a pickup. The first one in took repeated hits and was driven off by the intensity of the ground fire. The second managed to pick up the Hmong pilot while sustaining some battle damage. The Jollys dropped off the Hmong and headed home to Thailand. We all congratulated Bob on a job well done and drank an appropriate toast or two. It is what we did, our job.

In the morning we learned about the real world involving awards and decorations. The Jolly crews, who sat around our house all day, were bragging about how the pilot who did the pickup of the Hmong was being written up for the Air Force Cross, second only to the Medal of Honor. We were stunned, mostly at our own naiveté about what constituted "heroism" and the awarding of medals. We, I, were far too stringent

CHAPTER EIGHT

in writing people up for decorations basing that action on outstanding performance by our standards. Our standards, it seemed, were far more stringent about what constituted heroism. On the other hand, if you got medals as a Raven, you really earned them. I wrote Dunbar up for the Silver Star, which he received. Given the episode with the Jolly crew the previous month, and this exercise, we told the Jolly crews that they could pull their alert next to their helicopters and not in our house. They later stopped pulling alert at Long Tieng, but while they did they sat at the other end of the valley.

Dunbar did have another episode in which he, as a sort of joke, demanded a Distinguished Flying Cross. He was working along the North Vietnamese border in an O-1 with a backseater in place. He was about 70 miles from Long Tieng, in not very good weather conditions, when a massive thunderstorm started moving from west to east. He had just enough fuel to get home, about 50 minutes in the best of circumstances, and had no choice but to penetrate the broad based thunderstorm. Penetrating a thunderstorm is a dangerous maneuver to be avoided if at all possible, particularly in an airplane as light and slow as an O-1. Bob dutifully penetrated the mass of seething cloud and rain, doing his best to maintain level flight but it was not to be. The O-1 was hurled upward to over 12000 feet, rolling and tumbling in the process, and then dumped to down below the ridgelines he couldn't see. He went through this uncontrollable aerial rollercoaster experience several times before he finally broke free and made it home. Unfortunately, the backseater did not make this any easier by his prolonged projectile vomiting on Bob. It is amazing how a 120 pound person can puke that much. When Bob got up to the house as darkness settled in, completely covered with vomit, he slapped his hand on the bar and said, "I want a goddamn DFC, I earned it!" We all laughed and told him to go take a shower.

As time moved into October our new house next door got finished and we all moved around both houses and each of us had more space. My new room on the second floor of the new place had a window whose shutters (there was no glass) opened to a view of the bear cage about fifty feet away. Floyd, it must be said, put up with a lot of nonsense with a good sense of humor. More than once I saw somewhat tipsy case officers hug Floyd or give him light slaps. Floyd just hugged back. A Hmong soldier tried that once and Floyd ripped the guy's arm off at the elbow.

In the meantime, Cavanaugh left, Bill Kozma arrived, Mike Byers checked out in the T-28, one guy each from Luang Prabang (Al Daines) and Vientiane (Jerry Greven) were sent in to augment us, and more adventures were just on the horizon.

CHAPTER NINE

One might think that this series of negative events, despite the positives of battlefield success to this point, would have us sitting around our bar at night grousing about the actions, or inactions, of those above us in a rather murky chain. Our lives, however, ran at such a rapid pace in a danger-filled environment that almost every event passed by at great speed with little contemplation or reflection since the immediate horizon was filled with continuous challenges, any one of which could be lethal.

An observation about our lives was made to me recently by a retired CIA case officer. He pointed out that most people's lives, if put on a graph as a line, were mostly horizontal with occasional blips up and down. Our lives were a lot different, he said, with that line taking violent ups and downs, sometimes several times a day, sometimes off the chart and, if measured, would probably be three times the length of the normal near flat line of the ordinary person. We, he observed, have already lived three lifetimes. I think that is a good analogy. Put another way, the minds of most of us in the circumstances in which we operated very quickly sorted what could be done and how and when, what could not be done and why, and chose the path that was workable. While none of us could survive in this situation forever, those who could not process events in this fashion disintegrated early.

We had two more Ravens arrive that month, Terry Carroll and Henry Allen both of whom had experience as NAIL FAC out of NKP and added a lot of expertise to the business of finding trucks and where they hid. As an indicator of the flow of time in these sorts of situations, I felt like I worked with Terry and Henry for a long time. In reality, I left ten weeks later. Henry, near the end of his tour in 1970 went MIA and was later declared KIA. Terry took one look at our fireplace and the occasional rat problem and shook his head in wonderment at our lack of initiative. He took some measurements, went to the CIA supply guys, and manufactured a metal sheet plate that fit the bottom of the fireplace with a latched trap door that would dump the ashes. No rats, more heat, what can I say.

There were always interesting things to learn from the nightly social conversations we had at our house. Some of those things involved past relationships, such as Doc Quinby and I being in the same first grade class. Another sort of similar discovery was made when I found that Jerry Greven, our augmentee from Vientiane, had been in my ex-wife's high school class in Palo Alto, California. "You married who?", he said in chortling disbelief. My reply had something to do with him shutting up.

After a full day of flying I was in the comm room when one of the crew chiefs arrived and asked if I'd go back to the ramp with him since there were a couple of strangers down there and he wanted me to intervene. There were two guys wandering around, kind of sightseeing, so I approached them and asked who they were.

One guy introduced himself as Major Mike Carns, a Tiger fast FAC, and introduced his backseater whose name I do not remember. When I asked how they got here he replied that Andy Patten arranged it. My

CHAPTER NINE

reply was that was beyond Andy's authority and it was time to get off the ramp before someone else started asking questions.

Carns and the GIB (guy in back) may have been on a curiosity tour or they have been on some kind of muted apology visit but we, living our speedy life, didn't much care. We had an interesting time sitting around our bar and talking. We agreed, despite a policy against it, to take them on rides the next day. Ed Lauffer in an O-1 got the GIB, and I got Carns in the back of my T-28. We considered the T-28 to be a real speed demon compared to the O-1. With ordnance it cruised about 140 knots compared to 85 for the O-1. It had a limiting speed, with ordnance, of about 325 knots. It never dawned on me that the F-4 that Carns flew didn't get off the ground until it was doing 160.

The first target I worked that day with Carns in back was a supply dump and troop concentration hidden under moderate jungle cover. I explained to Carns that CIA intelligence had confirmed my previous observations. After checking it again, I climbed up to 5000 feet AGL, checked in the flight of four F-4, put down four WP and told them to "fill the box", Mark 82 first, then the CBU 24. I had zoomed back up to 5000 and then throttled back, beginning a slow descent while running the strike. The main purpose of this was to save as much fuel as possible since a T-28 gobbled 50 gallons an hour at a normal throttle setting. There was a modest amount of small arms fire that withered away as the CBU rained down.

Doing my usual, and much practiced, procedure, I zoomed (in my mind) through the target area at about 50 feet as the last F-4 pulled off. I had timed it right again and was now going to take a quick look at the results. Doing about 180 knots I did a damage estimate of the area. Carns, on interphone, made a kind of breathing noise that indicated that he didn't think this a brilliant move. That is where it became clear to me

163

that we had different speed perceptions. I put in a few more strikes and headed back to Long Tieng to drop off Carns before I got back to work.

The GIB, flying with Ed Lauffer, was absolutely astounded at what he could see from the back seat of an O-1 – and the visibility from the front seat is a lot better. We just smiled. That is what the O-1 was designed to do. In my second tour in SEA I flew the RF-4 and definitely learned the limitations of visual observation from a fast mover. I smoked a pipe in those days and Carns was kind enough to send me some pipe tobacco. We stayed in occasional touch over the years, often by accident, and he retired as the Vice Chief of Staff of the Air Force. There are those who say that he saved the Air Force from the very strange Chief of Staff when he was the Vice. I would say those observations are correct.

All of us, I am sure, at times suffered from amoebic dysentery resulting from our food and water sources. Early in October I started my second bout with this and the outcome was nearly fatal, not from the dysentery itself, which was bad enough, but from my self-medicated solution. I started self-dosing lomotil in what I later learned were near-fatal quantities, neutralized somewhat by my constant adrenalin rush. Among the side-effects not mentioned in medical literature is decreased depth perception and significantly lowered blood pressure. Not a good idea for a pilot. My first clue that something might be amiss was when I was strafing in a T-28 and a tree limb went over my head. The second clue came when I nearly became a smoking hole in the PDJ.

Among the pockets of NVA behind the friendly lines was a ZPU 14.5 mm positioned on the north western side of the PDJ. The gunners would blaze away at anything that they thought might be in range. We countered by staying out of range but one day they annoyed me a bit too much. I rolled into a 45 degree dive from 5000 feet AGL, lined up the combining glass sight, adjusted some as the ZPU tracer fire went ripping

CHAPTER NINE

over my head, and then fired two or three WP rockets that incinerated the gunners and possibly destroyed the gun. Then the fun started.

In a normal dive recovery in a T-28 you only pull 3.5 to 4 g which isn't much. You normally start to "gray out" at about 5.5 to 6 and black out around 7 – the blood being drained from your eyes by the g force overcoming the ability of your blood pressure to compensate. In this case I quickly grayed out and then, as the nose rose through the horizon, blacked out. I continued the pull up until I thought I was climbing about vertical and then neutralized the controls. My vision should have come back immediately but it didn't. I was blacked out blind. I could hear the sound of the wind noise lessening as the airplane reached a stall, probably about 5000 feet where I had started. Then the bird hammer-headed and flopped down and the wind noise increased as I brought the throttle to idle. My brain was telling me that this was the end unless somehow my body recovered quickly. Very gradually my sight grayed in to the point where I could just make out the ground that I was approaching rapidly. I gently recovered from the dive, not wanting to black out again. I would guess that I missed the ground by about a hundred feet. At the time I thought that maybe I was drinking too much scotch.

Mike Byers was working the Phou Na Kok area in the west end of Ban Ban Valley while I was working on the east end looking for more caves to blow shut with the flight of Thuds that would arrive in a few minutes. Mike suddenly got a call from Will Green saying that he and a squad of Hmong, operating outside their fortified compound, had just made contact with a company of NVA not more than 200 meters away. The only air we had available for the next 20 minutes or so was my flight of inbound Thuds. I called Mike and told him what was inbound and he called Green because there was a real problem here. Mike explained to Green that he had air inbound but that they were carrying pairs of 3000

MEETING STEVE CANYON

pound bombs that were far too dangerous to work that close to friendlies. Ever pragmatic Will replied, "..., consider the alternative...".

Mike briefed the Thuds on the situation, stressing the importance of accuracy. In a couple of minutes they dumped 12 tons of explosive on the hapless NVA company. Will said the NVA simply disappeared into an odd mist. Mike's adventures for the day were not over. He started having some kind of carburetor problem that much reduced the power of the engine, although it varied. He immediately started flying towards the PDJ following the road that led to the town of Khang Khai on the eastern edge of the PDJ. I quickly headed his direction in my T-28 but I was at least 12 miles behind him so it would take a while to catch up. In the meantime he had called Air America and a Huey was on the way to the eastern PDJ to make a pick up. Mike's O-1 almost touched down on the road a couple of times but he finally reached a patch of level grassy ground on the PDJ that was in a sort of no-man's land. He touched down, shut it down, and headed for the waiting Huey. I arrived in time to see them head for home. Another near miss.

The next day Frank Shaw got flown out to fix the O-1. Frank, like the rest of the maintenance guys, had not been in Vietnam. His eyes would widen when we would tell some of our Vietnam stories and his eyes must have really widened that day. Frank wasn't out there without some kind of friendlies around but his work got much faster when the worst sniper in NVA history started taking occasional potshots. All turned out well.

The 316th NVA Division had pretty much supplanted the battered 312th Division. The 316th had been in a protracted training environment in North Vietnam and it showed. We had destroyed a good part of their pre-positioned supplies – and we concentrated on destroying supplies and not "cutting" roads which was something of a fantasy. Route 7 runs into Laos from North Vietnam in the "Fishes Mouth" area. The road

CHAPTER NINE

enters Laos southeast of Ban Ban, turns north and then west descending into Ban Ban Valley. The road was built with steep sides, bare of vegetation, where it descended. Flying a T-28 in the area one day I noticed dark dots along the southern side of the road which, on closer examination, looked like holes. I got down low and flew directly at several of the holes, spraying them with machine gun fire. A couple of days later the CIA base chief in our nightly meeting asked if I had strafed those holes which, he informed me, was where road repair crews slept during the day. When I said yes he informed me that they were now digging L-shaped holes.

Much of the forward movement of NVA supplies was along trail networks running from the Fishes Mouth to the mostly destroyed town of Xieng Khoung. Supplies would get stored in various places along the way for incoming troops to carry forward. One of these places was what had been a village and still looked like one but, we knew, was not. I worked a pair of Thuds on this "village" one morning with pretty incredible results. I was in an O-1 and lead rolled in on my mark and dropped four Mark 82 on one side of the 43 structure complex. As I was about to direct two's first pass, the entire complex exploded, the concussion from exploding ammunition and fuel pushing my O-1 sideways with a violent push. Two aborted his pass, barely missing the gigantic fireball. All 43 structures were vaporized. I found somewhere else to use the rest of their ordnance.

Each of us saw the gaps in the 316th Division field knowledge based on their extended training status. My experience came one day as I was flying a T-28 to the northeast from the PDJ near where Route 7 exits from Ban Ban. There were several long ridge lines, perhaps 2 miles long, extending down towards Route 7 from the northwest. While flying along at maybe three thousand feet, minding my own business, one of the ridgelines lit up with ground fire. There had to be hundreds of muzzle flashes, but they weren't aimed at me. I looked around and there was a four ship of F-4 a bit ahead of and parallel to my heading and probably ten thousand feet above me.

The Vietnamese, certainly including these, were taught that an AK-47 can shoot down a fast mover. That is true, but they have to be really low and really close for AK-47 fire to be effective. These guys were the victims of training overkill. They soon became victims of another sort. I called Cricket and got a four ship of F-4. When I rolled in to mark a "box" around what had to be a battalion, they opened up again making it all the more graphic for the fighters. I stayed low on my dive recovery and flew past many NVA troops blazing away at the F-4. The massive CBU explosions melded with the muzzle flashes. It would be reasonable to assume that most of that battalion was killed.

The establishment of the "Raven boxes" had pretty much restricted the fast FAC to the road network. They would attack any trucks they could find, "cut" and mine roads with a couple of kinds of ordnance, and hit any targets outside the Raven boxes that they or 7th Air Force deemed worthwhile. The NVA would typically run truck convoys at night, with some exceptions, and hide the trucks under jungle canopy alongside major roads such as Route 7. They would truck supplies as far as western Ban Ban Valley and then porter the supplies forward from there. There was also a significant amount of portering going on through the valleys that ran from the Fishes Mouth ended to near the town of Xieng Khoung and on to the southern PDJ area. Determining porter routes, and the status of the villages through which they ran, particularly on the southern route, was a difficult to impossible process without the intelligence support and sense of the battlefield which we possessed. Many of the villages had been abandoned as a flood of refugees streamed towards the PDJ. We would strike "villages" that we knew had become merely

CHAPTER NINE

storage facilities, and avoid those we knew were still villages. We could only hope that fast FAC who might be watching did not draw the wrong conclusions.

In one episode there definitely was a fast FAC, a LAREDO from Udorn, watching when Mike Byers worked a strike on a very foolish daytime convoy on Route 7 southeast of Ban Ban. The strike destroyed all 13 trucks in the convoy and Mike went on to do other things. Truck kills were an important measure of achievement for regular Air Force pilots so what followed was sort of understood by us, in a laughable way. Mike was working in the area the next day when the same Laredo came back and worked a set of fighters on the truck carcasses remaining from the strike Mike had run the previous day. And the Laredo came back for a total of five straight days pounding the same wreckage over and over. The fighter pilots had to have been blind to not see that what they were attacking was scrap metal. 65 trucks "killed" by that Laredo – must have made an impression at Udorn.

Shortly after this I was working a pair of A-1 on a NVA troop formation on the eastern PDJ, well within a Raven Box. I was in a T-28 and we were working the strike pattern at about 5000 feet AGL because of heavy small arms and 12.7 fire, and possibly some ZPU. I had marked and the A-1 were working when I saw a solitary F-4, engine smoke trailing, coming right towards our orbit. After making a warning call we all split-essed down into the ground fire and immediately began climbing to get out of it.

I called Cricket and asked what fast FAC was in the area and what was his freq? After their reply I switched to that UHF freq and called the LAREDO repeatedly. It had to be the same 65 truck kill idiot. No reply. We began working again and here he came again. We split-essed again into the ground fire and climbed back to pattern altitude. My repeated calls, including those made on the Guard emergency frequency (243.0) got no response. We went back to work and here he came again. Having had all the nonsense I could stand, I armed up my two .50 cals and did a quick burst of about 50 rounds in front of his nose as he flew through our formation. He immediately came up on the UHF freq I had previously called, and marveled at the ground fire. I said, "That wasn't ground fire, asshole, you come through here again and I'll shoot you down". He didn't reply and left the area. Getting killed by the bad guys was part of the equation. Getting killed by the so-called friendlies because of their incompetence was another story.

All this contributed to a flow of Johnnie Walker and stories at our bar after the sun went down and we mentally prepped for the next day. Having been back in the saddle for three months I was finding the mental prep process to be getting more difficult. One part of my brain seemed to be telling me to do things that I knew were not very bright, while another part of my brain seemed to be leaning back and wondering why I was doing those things. I do not know if what I recognized to be fraying around my edges was visible to the others, but it was becoming visible to me. In the meantime, we had visitors of one sort or another.

The first visitors were a delegation from Switzerland, of all places. The Pilatus Porter was made in Switzerland and was a critical element in the Air America and Continental fleets. The Swiss, acting under political pressure I am sure, were visiting to assure someone that the airplanes they made were not being used for some violent purpose. As part of a Kabuki dance, the Swiss visited Sam Thong, across Skyline Ride from Long Tieng, which was civilian oriented in its activities. They were then transported out to Lima Lima on the PDJ for whatever purpose. They were accompanied, unknown to me at the time, by US news types. We were instructed not to conduct airstrikes within their sight.

CHAPTER NINE

There was a NVA troop concentration about seven miles west-northwest of Lima Lima that I was going to hit with a pair of A-1, but the target area was too close to Lima Lima. The three of us orbited around about ten miles west for what seemed like an eternity. I finally called the case officer frequency at Lima Lima and a Hmong assistant answered. I asked if the visitors were still there and he said they were gone. Great! I led the A-1 to the target area, checked in with the local Hmong commander and started working the A-1. Within seconds the case officer called. "They're still here you dumbshit"! Okay, okay the cat was out of the bag but we went away and hit something out of sight. Ten years later I was watching an ABC 20/20 segment on the war in Laos and there I was on camera with my voice running the strike. Oops!

I came back later in the afternoon in a T-28 and, with the radio direction of the guide on the ground, eliminated the NVA troops with WP.

A message came in from the AIRA office ordering Cavanaugh to appear that night at the AIRA house to be part of a cocktail party/light dinner for two visiting Senate Foreign Relations Committee staffers – Mr. Walter Pincus and Mr. Paul. The AIRA office didn't seem to be on top of things since Cavanaugh had been gone for about a week. I was an acceptable substitute so after that day's work I cleaned up and flew a T-28 south.

After parking the airplane I took one of the jeeps to Colonel Tyrell's house. Coming inside and walking into the living room I was struck by the look on Mrs. Tyrell's face when we were introduced. Her expression seemed to say that the Huns had come to town and she would be the first molested, or something. It seemed that CIA would not permit Pincus and Paul to visit 20A so my job was to describe to them what went on there, excluding sensitive subjects. They were lucky Cavanaugh was gone. I was also instructed to "make them cry". Paul was there but

MEETING STEVE CANYON

Pincus was expected to arrive at Wattay soon, returning from Savannakhet. I was instructed to drive out to the airport and pick him up.

It was just dark when the Continental C-46 landed and pulled up to the terminal ramp. I pulled the jeep around to behind the wing and in front of the door to receive the solitary passenger, Walter Pincus. He was covered in puke from the roots of his hair to the soles of his shoes. I was more than taken aback and asked him how this had happened as he got in the jeep and I drove away. He explained that he had been given a ride by a Raven, with Colonel Tyrell's agreement, who showed him what that place down south was like and how the job worked. This seemed a bit odd to me as I drove Pincus to where he was staying so he could clean up and change his clothes. I later found out from the Raven, Tom Verso, that he, like the rest of us, considered Congressional staffers to be one step above journalists in the ladder out of the slime pit. He had done everything possible in his O-1, short of ripping the wings off. Walter Pincus, by the way, is an excellent journalist who writes insightful and realistic columns for the Washington Post.

We finally got back to the Tyrell's house, drank some, ate some, drank some more and I did get Pincus and Paul to cry. Their mission, it seemed, was to gather data for Senator Fulbright, chairman of the committee, to help block the introduction of regular US forces into Laos. They must have been living in some fantasy world back there, given the state of the anti-war movement and societal fractionalization at the time. Having done my job, a former Thud pilot on Tyrell's staff, and his wife, drove me to the staff house where I could get some sleep before taking off at first light.

Our next visitor was far more important, considering our environment, and provided a revealing view of command thinking. General George S. Brown, commander of 7th Air Force, arrived at Long Tieng in an Air America Volpar early one afternoon. The CIA base chief, using our

CHAPTER NINE

map room, gave an informal but thorough presentation on the situation, realities of the area, and a short-term projection of things to come. I stood there silently with my AK-47 and bandolier slung over my right shoulder, another Raven at my side. Brown acknowledged our presence but said nothing. "How many people do you have up here, Tom?", he said. Tom took a puff on his Cuban cigar, nodded and said about 15 Air Force now, so a bit less than 40 total, not including Air America". Brown seemed slightly surprised when he replied, "Hell, we'd have a hundred thousand up here." "Yes", nodded Tom, taking another puff, "and you'd lose your ass." Brown, an excellent politician, showed no sign of irritation.

"You know, Tom", he continued in an even tone, "I'm not sure I like Lieutenants and Captains running their own war". Tom nodded, took a puff, and said, "Well George, they're the only people we've met from the Air Force who know what the fuck they're doing". We couldn't applaud but the thought was there. "You may have a point there, Tom", Brown concluded with a tight-lipped smile. The other Raven and I left to walk down the hill to the runway, there being no jeeps available. Brown went past in the back of a captured Soviet command vehicle and waved. We waved back. His Volpar departed before we took off.

Brown's remarks were a nice way of confirming what we already knew, at least those of us that paid attention. The big Air Force did not like us and it was a control issue to them, not a results issue. In recent years I have read more about this situation and found that General Brown, and others, were very disturbed and somewhat heated about the role the Ravens played in the use of airpower. There are numerous references citing General Brown, and Army General Abrams the MACV commander, as believing that CIA and the US Embassy in Laos "know nothing" and just "dumped bombs in the jungle". I am sure that they actually believed that, even as they ignored the huge fallacies in their existing pre-plan and target assignment process – a farce with which we had extensive experience.

The reality, of course, is that those labels applied to them and they had demonstrated that over and over again. I have written repeatedly in this book about the intelligence support received by the Ravens for good reason. The command structure in our situation, the CIA, knew their objective, they knew that airpower was key to achieving that objective, and they provided the Ravens, the means of airpower application, with the information and intelligence necessary to effectively apply airpower with precision at the time and place it was needed. The decision-action cycle could run from 12 hours to five minutes, and the action taken was usually done with accuracy. Looking back, it does make one wonder about the perceptions that guided the top of that military command chain.

Late one afternoon Joe Potter and I were on the concrete deck near the bear cage talking with the CIA base chief and his boss, the Chief of Station (COS). Shortly after Joe and I walked up the base chief, with an appropriately sad look on his face, informed Joe that he was sorry but they had just received a report that a T-28 had been shot down and there were no survivors. Joe didn't blink an eye and replied in an even voice that he was sorry too since Igor was in the back seat. The base chief nearly fainted and the COS eyebrows peaked.

Igor was one of the CIA communications specialists and he really, really wanted to go for a T-28 ride. Mike Byers had finally relented and they were flying when this conversation was going on. The real problem here was that CIA personnel were not to do things that could get them captured or killed, particularly if it was not in their job description. Doing so by a subordinate was also bad for the supervisor. About the time the parties to this conversation were considering what to say next, Igor came

CHAPTER NINE

walking towards the bear cage, all smiles. While the COS and base chief did not exactly lunge at him, I'm sure it was a professional ass-chewing for Igor.

Andy Patten would visit periodically, fly with some of us, and generally estimate where our physical and emotional states were in regard to well-being and survivability. We went for a T-28 ride, Andy in the back seat, and he would occasionally do the flying. He orbited the east end of Ban Ban in, I think, an effort to gauge my reaction. As we started into his third orbit I tersely told him that this wasn't a good place to fly in circles. After giving him a tour we landed back at Long Tieng. Andy didn't order you to do things, but he told me I needed to go on R&R. I agreed and he set me up for Australia in a couple of days.

We now had nine Ravens working ABOUT FACE so I only felt slightly guilty about leaving, and it was something each of us needed to do from time to time. The day before I ferried an O-1 to Udorn and left for Australia, I worked nine airstrikes and 31 sorties. The BDA from that day included dozens of secondary fires and explosions, some of them massive. All of us were experiencing a heavier level of warfare.

Getting to Australia and getting back took 12 days and it was not without a little excitement, of sorts. My dysentery problem had gone away so I felt comfortable about that situation. The C-130 Thailand commuter flight, the "Klong", dropped me in Bangkok and I quickly processed through for the Pan Am flight to Saigon and Camp Alpha. There were a group of fighter pilots on board and we had time to chat and were all delighted with the lunch provided – turkey sandwiches with lots of mayonnaise. Sounds great but eating mayo in Thailand, at least then, was a really bad idea. We would discover how bad. A bunch of us from that Pan Am flight got on the World Airways flight to Sydney the next day and then the problem presented itself. Mayonnaise in Thailand was typically not stored correctly and often picked up bacteria that led to intestinal problems. Sure enough, about the time we leveled off those of us who had been on the Pan Am flight were standing in line twitching and crossing our legs. Fortunately, everything was deposited in the appropriate places. Just what I needed.

I was seated next to a Navy Lieutenant who was a port officer at Vung Tao in South Vietnam and was getting out of the Navy to go to law school. We chatted for a bit and then drifted off to sleep. He would have an amazing story on our return trip.

This time in Australia was quiet with most of my time hanging around Sydney, taking tours, eating and drinking. I had a sort of internal sense that I was supposed to be somewhere else and doing something else and that all this was somehow not appropriate. That is not an easy sensation to ignore. The six and a half days (not seven because then you could get married after seven days in Australia) ended soon enough and I was back on World Airways and sitting next to the Navy guy. His R&R was very different.

He played golf and after a number of holes the older Australian he was playing with asked him what he did in the Navy and the Lieutenant said he was currently a port officer in South Vietnam but before that he had been an assistant engineering officer on the USS Boston. The Australian dropped his golf club and stared at the Lieutenant open-mouthed. Finally, he told his story. He had been in the Australian Army in World War II and during the battle for Bougainville he had been so badly wounded that the Australians had left him for dead. American medics, however, saw that he wasn't dead and transported him to the USS Boston where the surgeons saved his life.

The Australian insisted that the Lieutenant come home with him for drinks and dinner, which is what he did. It turned out the Australian had

CHAPTER NINE

lots of money and a beautiful daughter who took an instant liking to the Lieutenant. "So", I asked, "what next"? "Well", he replied, "I've been accepted at the law school of the University of New South Wales and I think I've met my future wife". A lot can happen in six and a half days. I hope worked well for them both.

I worked four strikes the afternoon of the day I returned to Long Tieng. Not much had changed other than a finely growing intensity. The friendlies kept capturing AAA guns, particularly 37 mm, but it didn't cut the ground fire at all. At this point they had captured 77 37 mm guns. That evening the base chief gave me another special mission to do in the morning.

"At 0700 tomorrow", he said, "a special seven truck convoy will cross the North Vietnamese border on Route 7. The third truck and everything in it must be destroyed". You didn't ask why or what was in the truck, you just did it.

I took off before 0630 so that I would be in the area on time, or a bit before. Climbing to about 4000 AGL I watched the landscape slide past. Soon, Ban Ban valley appeared at about ten o'clock and I altered course to the right slightly, crossed Route 7 on the southeast side of Ban Ban and edged over to a 50 square mile patch of nearly deserted, relatively open, real estate from which the road could be seen as it snaked eastward into North Vietnam. It was 0652 and there were no trucks visible.

It was time to look preoccupied for the benefit of the promised special seven truck convoy, which must have been desperate to make this run in daylight. I pushed the mixture to rich, set so-called combat power of 36 inches over 2400 rpm, and called HOTPLATE, a Hmong recon team in the area, on 125.3 VHF.

"Hotplate, Raven four-five. You hear my engine?"

The response was almost immediate. Hotplate lived a perilous life on the run, supplied by Air America, constantly watching and reporting, constantly pursued. I didn't want to hit him with my minor demonstration. "Ah, Raven, you way sou't a me."

Good enough. I clicked my mike button twice. Hotplate knew not to be chatty, the NVA would DF him (direction find) -- to a useful accuracy if he did. I moved my left hand to the arming panel on the lower edge of the instrument panel and switched the over-center MASTER ARM switch to ON. A cross-and-ladder sight picture blossomed brightly on the combining glass of the sight. Turning down the brightness to a dull whiteness, I set in 42 mils sight depression, toggled number one station up to ON for rockets and moved the GUNS switch to SAFE. Pneumatics blew back the breeches on both guns, sending an almost erotic shudder through the airplane. Moving the switch to ARM, the first round in each belt chambered with another erotic surge of compressed air. There was a seam in the wing a couple of feet out from the fuselage that was a handy reference mark for a thirty degree dive angle. Sliding up to the left seam were some old hootches 3000 feet below, long abandoned by villagers caught in the crush of war. Sunlight streamed over the ridges, dappling the greenness of fields and jungle.

I rolled the Tango nearly inverted and pulled down until the sight cross slid under the center hootch. Rolling upright, I let the cross climb up to the hootch, corrected a bit for the surface wind seen moving the trees, the airspeed climbed towards a release at 250 knots, sounds of wind and engine tugged at the senses. There ... experience said we've reached release speed, angle, and altitude ... my right thumb pressed the button midway up the stick and one WP rocket with its 28 pound warhead swooshed out of the number one LAU-7 pod. The rocket, almost instantly supersonic, reached out to the hootch in a couple of

CHAPTER NINE

seconds and hit the front porch, obliterating the old structure with an 80 foot flaming burst of phosphorus burning at several thousand degrees. Up, up in a gentle three to four G pull, I turned right and looked over at the road a couple of miles away.

There, on time, came seven trucks racing down Route 7 at an almost dangerous speed of 45 mph or more. They appeared to be unimpressed by a solitary T-28D off to their right, beating up on some unknown target. I reversed the turn, rolled back in on the burning hootch, set the mils to 10 for strafing, picked up speed in a steep dive, bottomed out at a hundred feet AGL maybe 400 yards from the hootch, and pulled the trigger. The two fifties juddered and roared with stunning ferocity for a couple of seconds, the ball ammo tracers disappearing into the center of the flames. I pulled up, over the hootch, high up in a lazy chandelle to where there was some visibility. The trucks were still barreling down the road, starting to slide behind the rising terrain leading up to a 6200 foot mountain, around which Route 7 turns north. Getting down on the back side of the slope to hide the sound of the airplane, I let experience tell me where they'd be when I popped over the ridge to hunt down the third truck. Engine heat poured back into the cockpit, tree tops flowed past with a glassy green blur just beneath the gray wings, the ridge beckoned, the ridge receded, and there they are about 500 yards ahead. Staying close to the ground, I got level with the third truck about 1200 feet out. The sight got reset to 20 mils.

Station one was still selected. The cross drifted up over the third truck, closer now, maybe 1000 feet, green AK tracer slashed from the following trucks. I screwed up with a 45 degree off-axis shot but you have to take what you've got. My thumb pushed out a rocket. It was going to be a miss ahead. One second gone and I'm 250 feet closer, I kicked rudder, centered the needle and ball. It looked good so I fired again, again. A second later

179

two WP warheads slammed into the third truck which, a half second later, disappeared in an inferno no thing or person could survive. I popped over the blazing hulk at 20 feet and dropped into the valley beyond, turned left beyond their sight, picked up some speed and came back for more.

The picture on the road had changed a lot in the 45 seconds or so that it took to rack the Tango around uphill and get it flat on the road chasing trucks. It was spooky down there amongst them, and not a life-extending practice. The tree line and dirt road rushed past in a blur, my eyes only focused ahead through the windscreen. The engine bellowed with the power of an aviation age gone by. The third truck was a hulk, but the other six were running wild down the two-lane dirt road, or looking for a place to hide. There was no chance to get them all.

Number seven didn't see the Tango, almost level with his tailgate. Firing intuitively now, a two second burst from the fifties shuddered the airplane, bushel-basket sized blue flame spouted from the gun barrels. The orange tracers reached out, chewed the truck to pieces, and flame gouted from the ruptured fuel tank. Up and over, keeping the prop off the dirt, I missed the fireball, and looked for six . He was running down an incline and into the trees, never mind. Number five was trying to pass number four, my rocket hit short blinding the next shot, I fired anyway and missed again. The resident gunners alongside the road had the range and 12.7mm and 14.5 mm ZPU tore past in odd green-white sheets streaking out from the tree lines. A bulky, oblong truck was coming up fast when a trigger pull sent two seconds of fifty cal tearing from aft to front. The truck seemed to slow, swerving in death. It burned convulsively as I pulled up over it and slithered to safety over the trees. That was one for the customer and two for me. That was the only special mission that involved that much extra drama and color. Part of me hoped there would be more.

CHAPTER TEN

By early November the friendlies had advanced about as far as they were going to go, with minor exceptions. They were on the edge of the old French administrative center at Khang Khai on the eastern PDJ, which is not to say that there weren't active pockets of NVA west of there behind our lines. The hills just southeast of Khang Khai would soon fall to the friendlies. The southern PDJ was fairly secure but with a limited projection down Route 4 towards the battered town of Xieng Khoung. Phou Na Kok, east of Route 7 where it exited Ban Ban Valley remained an island in a violent sea experiencing daily ground assaults. Across Route 7 from this position the NVA supply porters were taking a tremendous beating as they moved supplies towards the PDJ and the NVA forces that still dominated the Route 7/71 road junction area. The west and northwest PDJ area, particularly in the foothills, still held good-sized NVA units.

Our focus continued to be on destroying supplies and engaging NVA troops, although there were occasional odd side experiences. One day, based on CIA intelligence sources, Mike Byers eliminated the "leftist neutralist" headquarters in the Fishes Mouth area. I don't think any of us realized that there was such a thing as "leftist neutralists" but we wondered if they were as wimpy as the rightest neutralists. If so, we should have ignored them since they would have been a major irritant to the NVA.

The 316th Division troops continued to make absurd tactical errors for which they paid a steep price. One day they tried to assault the Phu Na Kok site by coming in from an unanticipated direction, in this case a very steep hillside that was almost cliff-like. It was very hard going for a company-sized unit to struggle up through the heavy vegetation and they started making noise in the process. This attracted the quiet attention of the friendlies who told the case officer who called me on VHF. Working a strike flight on the NVA troops would not be a good idea since the slightest error would result in friendly casualties. I rolled my T-28 level with the mottled green vegetation that masked the NVA and blanketed the area with WP. That took care of that problem.

This sort of near-total destruction of enemy forces happened at a more than expected rate and sometimes without our knowledge at the time. At one evening meeting a couple of us read an intercept that indicated that three bloodied survivors of a 500 man battalion had staggered into a regimental command post to report what had happened to the battalion during an airstrike. One of us had directed the strike but the outcome didn't seem to match anything we knew.

As the airstrip at Lima Lima became active, a flood of refugees arrived for transport away from the battle area that, for them, had been a battle area for a very long time. This flood must have had some encouragement of some sort by Vang Pao but, in any event, there were something like 6000 refugees airlifted out by Air America and taken to safer places. When I would land at Lima Lima to refuel and rearm I would sometimes look at the refugees lined up for quick interviews before they got onto the waiting C-123 aircraft. Most of them looked in adequate physical condition but one middle aged male certainly stood out. His abdomen had

CHAPTER TEN

been clipped by bomb or shell fragments and I could see his intestines while he was holding them in place with one hand. It is possible that he survived that, but it would be a long shot given the environment.

Khang Khai had a series of two floor red-tile roofed buildings that had previously been part of a French administrative complex. There was a "Chinese Cultural Mission" located there whose presence imposed a "no bomb" circle around the small area. We did not bomb the place, since that would leave evidence, but we would occasionally pitch some CBU in that direction. I doubt that the Chinese or anyone else walked around during the day. The Chinese were, of course, not there for cultural reasons but as advisors. Who they were advising is a bit of a mystery to me since I doubt the Vietnamese would be much interested and the Pathet Lao were pretty well tied to the Vietnamese. In any event the Chinese staff fled Khang Khai in October and started the hike back to North Vietnam. They were ambushed by a Hmong patrol and the ranking Chinese, a Colonel, was killed much to the fury of CIA who really wanted to have a long talk with the Colonel.

The friendly presence in Khang Khai was somewhat marginal and it was not safe enough for CIA to let us up close which is unfortunate. There is a cemetery there that I am sure contains the graves of a number of Americans but it was in a contested area at the time. Post-war MIA recovery teams have not gone grave-digging for fear of offending the Hmong. The other items of interest were two buried arms caches. These consisted of very large numbers of infantry type weapons buried in two locations. I recall there being something like 9000 weapons in one and 7000 in the second, but that is just a recollection. What happened to the weapons was interesting to watch.

After being unearthed and cleaned up a bit they were transported the few miles to Lima Lima where multiple Air America C-123 transports

MEETING STEVE CANYON

hauled them away to somewhere. This did not happen quickly so during several refueling stops I got to watch the process. There was a fairly short Caucasian directing which weapons went to which aircraft. I was close enough for each of us to see each other and he certainly was not one of the CIA guys. Thirteen years later, while living in Northern Virginia, I needed a part for a Walther P-38 my father had brought back from World War II. The only authorized Walther distributor in the United States was a company named Interarms located in Alexandria. There had long been rumors about a relationship between CIA and Interarms and the owner, Sam Cummings.

I went to the Interarms location along the Alexandria waterfront in what appeared to be a bunch of interconnected townhouses and warehouses. A secretary directed me to a waiting room where an Interarms representative arrived a few minutes later. It was the guy from the PDJ and my face must have registered recognition since he gave me a look saying he would deny anything I said.

Another example of Vang Pao's ability to see the near future happened about then. I had refueled and rearmed an O-1 but had some slack time. VP asked if I'd like to get in his jeep with two soldiers and drive to the Khang Khai area. I immediately accepted and we drove away but after a couple of hundred yards VP held up his hand for the driver to stop. He looked at me and said, "not today". We turned around and went back to Lima Lima. I took off and followed the road towards Khang Khai. Where the road went through some forested hills just west of the town there was an NVA ambush in position, waiting. They got more than they expected.

One morning a bit after dawn I came down to the T-28 I was to fly and found Frank Shaw dozing on the gravel under a wing. This was not unusual and Frank opened his sleep-puffy eyes when he heard me

CHAPTER TEN

coming and got to this feet. "I want to show you something", he said while leading me towards the tail of the T-28. Forward of the tail and behind the rear seat there is a door on the bottom of the fuselage that swings down. This permits maintenance inspections and is also a place to stow baggage. We both stood in the door opening, the fuselage reaching down to our waist area. Frank shined a flashlight on the elevator cable that ran aft on the left side of the fuselage, and on a radio rack that was mounted just above the elevator cable. He showed me that he had found the cables, fore and aft, resting on the radio rack where someone who knew what they were doing had placed them. It didn't take a lot of strength but you did have to know what you were doing. He wanted me to get in the cockpit and move the stick to see if I could feel the extra resistance.

I moved the stick a few times and it seemed normal. Frank showed me the shavings off the seven wire cable from that minor amount of friction. We would never know how long it would take for the cable to be worn through and fail, but it would fail in flight. If the cable failed in level flight it was possible to land at a large flat airfield somewhere, but not Long Tieng, if you were skillful and lucky. If you were in a dive you would be dead. Another something to think about.

Joe Potter had a great deal of time in the T-28 and had given me a number of tips about the airplane, tips that were not in the flight manual. One of those was how to get maximum range in a minimum fuel situation. Late one afternoon I got to put Joe's advice to the test.

The fuel low-level warning light in the T-28 illuminated when the fuel level got down to 200 pounds – about 30+ gallons. That was about 45 minutes of flying time at a reduced cruise power setting. I was working a pair of A-1 on the hills north of Route 7 on the PDJ when the warning light came on. I ignored it since I wasn't finished and there was plenty of fuel to get home. I finished with the A-1 and headed back to Long Tieng showing 120 pounds on the fuel gauge. About that time I got a call from Cricket that Long Tieng weather was too bad for an approach. I asked if a Raven there had reported the weather, since we knew ways to sneak in, so they checked. In a minute or so I was informed that it was indeed a Raven that said there was no way home. I turned right to the northwest and headed for Luang Prabang, the Royal capitol, not knowing exactly where it was and having very little fuel left. Then I remembered Joe's advice and pulled the prop control back to 1600 RPM and boosted the throttle to 26 inches of manifold pressure while starting a very gentle climb to 10000 feet.

Someone had once mentioned a rough heading and distance from Moung Soui to Luang Prabang but that wasn't exactly the basis for precise navigation. The immediate future wasn't exactly brilliant since "LP", as we called it, was pretty well surrounded by NVA/PL troops so bailing out near them was not a good idea but it might be the only choice. Then another idea popped up. I called Cricket and got a frequency for the airborne-radar equipped EC-121 that droned around in what had to be a very boring job monitoring aircraft movement. After making contact I turned on the old, simple, and never used Mode 3 transponder in the T-28. The EC-121 immediately gave me a new heading, 15 degrees off what I had been flying, and a range of 17 miles. Telling them they could take credit for a "save", I adjusted accordingly and landed at LP just before the field was closed for weather. The fuel gauge showed about 20 pounds and the next morning I didn't ask how much fuel it took to fill the tanks. My knees were shaking a bit when the AOC, Don Moody, picked me up in his jeep and took me to their house. It had been a near miss and I could definitely feel my sense of invulnerability crumbling.

A few days later, after a normal day at work, it was my turn to take a battle-damaged RLAF T-28 to Udorn for repair. As they did far too often,

CHAPTER TEN

the Hmong pilots set their bomb fuses for two seconds separation (the time from bomb release until it is armed) instead of the standard six seconds. This allowed them to get closer to the target with more accuracy but also put them far too close to the bomb blast. The T-28 I was to ferry south was an example of this with 85 holes in the skin, one of them a foot across. All the holes were sealed with "speed tape", sort of a classier version of duct tape. A maintenance guy would ride in the back seat so he could get a couple of nights off in Udorn. It would be a more interesting flight than we desired.

It was a few minutes before sundown when we descended to traffic pattern altitude a few miles from Udorn and I switched over to tower frequency. The radio was pure chaos. A few seconds before I switched to tower freq an F-4 had landed with a hung bomb which fell off the F-4, bounced down the runway and detonated. The tower operator told everyone to go hold somewhere while they sorted things out. Air America and Continental were coming home to roost and somewhere there were fast movers who needed to land and things were confusing. I edged farther south and lower, trying to get away from the increasing numbers of slow movers circling in the twilight that was quickly going dark. Below me I spotted a lit swimming pool and wondered how that could be. The guy in back said it was some US Army place but it seemed very weird. I was down to a few hundred feet orbiting the swimming pool when I decided it was time to go to Vientiane. A few years later when I worked in intelligence systems in the Pentagon I discovered that this was Ramasun Station, a HF intercept facility that was part of a global network. When I asked what two T-28 engine magnetos at low altitude would do to reception I was told that it would really screw things up.

We arrived at Vientiane, parked the airplane, the maintenance guy disappeared, and I took a jeep to the attaché staff house for a place to sleep and hopefully get some food. I arrived at the house in time for a quick drink and sat down to dinner with ten or so downtowners. The main course that night was extremely good roast beef served, by a couple of house staff, with everything that was supposed to be there. It was incredibly beyond my imagination after a couple of months of our scrounging for food. When the roast beef serving plate arrived at where I was sitting there were two slices left. I took them both.

The downtowner sitting to my left sneeringly declared that I was "... certainly being selfish since someone else might want some...". My reply was that I was sure that there was plenty more in the kitchen. He then said, in the same haughty tone, that "... we are sick and tired of you people whining about not having a cook...". I finished my dinner and left before I did something nasty, now fully understanding why we had to leave our guns at the airport.

Joe Potter was in town and somehow I hooked up with him and we spent way too much time drinking. I quietly slipped into my assigned bed a bit before three and left shortly after six and headed for the airport with a severe hangover. The weather was not very good but I took off anyway for the 30 mile trip to Udorn, flying instruments much of the way and having to make a precision radar approach. I turned in the airplane and found a place to nap at a fighter squadron before ferrying an O-1 to Long Tieng.

About that time CIA informed us that they had found two Thai cooks for us and that they would arrive in a few weeks after their background checks were complete. None of us, to my knowledge, had asked CIA to find us cooks – they just did it. I also suspect that they might have done so because they didn't want us hanging around their dining room, which a few of us had been doing. The thoughts that most of us had at the time do not need any description. In later years the Air

CHAPTER TEN

Force made written comments about us not understanding for whom we worked, the Air Force in their mind, and how we had not demonstrated appropriate loyalty upwards. Those sorts of comments generate a bit of contempt.

The fast FAC, as previously suggested, seemed to sometimes think that they were impervious to the realities of our environment because, well, they were fast and modern, or something. On numerous occasions we had watched them zipping along at very low altitude, apparently thinking they were immune to the wave of ground fire that was following them. One LAREDO fast FAC from Udorn told me that 37 mm couldn't shoot him down because it was, after all, a World War II era weapon. He got a life lesson a bit later when, racing around Ban Ban, a 37 mm put a round up his right engine exhaust, exploding in the engine bay.

The aircraft streaming fire, he headed for the general area of Long Tieng and got a couple of miles south of our valley when he and the GIB punched out just before the aircraft exploded. The Jolly Greens on alert at Long Tieng had a minute or so of warning and were slogging through their ponderous checklists. In the meantime, Mike Byers took off in a T-28 to provide any necessary cover for the Air America Huey that was heading for the F-4 crew. The Jolly Greens were starting to taxi when the Huey and Mike Byers returned to Long Tieng with the rescued crew. We admonished them for their foolishness and put them on the next shuttle to Udorn.

The air support available at night consisted of RLAF AC-47 gunships, A-1 two-ship formations, and occasional solo A-26 aircraft. These aircraft, communicating through ALLEY CAT the night ABCCC, would work directly with the Hmong Forward Air Guides at each Lima Site. The CIA case officers who worked the sites during the day were forbidden to be out there at night. The chances of capture were greater and the chances of intervention or rescue were slim.

MEETING STEVE CANYON

Very late one afternoon I was working around Phu Na Kok where there were repeated TIC situations. Working into the darkness was not fun, mostly because it meant going back to land my T-28 on an unlit runway in a dark and narrow valley. I was working via VHF with Will Green, the site case officer who was African-American and had a distinctive radio voice. I didn't say anything but it was dark and he was still there and he was not supposed to be. The friendlies used mortar illumination rounds as I worked a pair of Thuds on the last of the enemy troops, strafing them as one last goodbye. It was really dark as I headed back to Long Tieng, some 40 miles away. The maintenance guys had parked a Jeep at the far end of the runway and turned the lights on when I made my radio call. While there were lights in the part of the valley where the Americans and VP were, there were none on the runway. I flew an overhead pattern, maintaining very precise control over airspeed and altitude, and made a good touchdown. It was my fourth and last night landing there and all of them were very stressful.

I took a jeep up to the house, ready for a drink after another long and tough day. I walked into our bar and there was Will Green. This was not possible. There was no Air America airplane that could have lifted him out of Phu Na Kok and got him to our bar in time to finish half a drink. I idled up and poured myself a drink, leaning close to Will and asking quietly him how he beat me back from Phu Na Kok. He looked at me as if I had completely lost my mind. We went over things a couple of times and then he nodded, smiling. "You were talking to my interpreter. I taught him English and he sounds just like me". It was a reasonable explanation and interesting. Somewhere in the United States, one hopes, there is a Lao (not Hmong) with a distinctive accent that doesn't sound like any other Lao.

While we saw much more of the gruesome side of war than most others in the Air Force, we did not often see the blood and gore so famil-

CHAPTER TEN

iar to infantry. When you do it will leave a lasting memory and spark thoughts that will remain with you. It is also a reminder that you too are vulnerable. Early one afternoon I walked down to the airfield where my O-1 for the day was parked. Hmong custom required the return of bodies to families if it all possible. An Air America pilot had hauled bodies back from the battlefield but did not use good judgment where he offloaded his cargo.

There were 20 or more bodies laid out on the asphalt parking area near Vang Pao's house and across the runway from our parking area. The bodies exhibited the mass trauma of war. Brains spilled out from head shots, intestines leaked out from ripped abdomens, some arms and legs were missing, and there was blood on all of them. Their relatives – wives, children, parents – keened and moaned, screamed with grief, and some collapsed next to their departed kin wishing to follow or wishing to bring them back but there would be no return. I stood there for a few minutes, my shouldered AK-47 and map bag, weighing on my shoulders, my mind processing the scene and weighing the costs of war to these people. Clenching my teeth I walked across the runway to my O-1 where a small group of maintenance guys watched the bodies and families in a horrified silence. We made the Vietnamese pay every day but today I vowed to make them pay even more.

There was a Lt Colonel intelligence officer in the AIRA office who came to Long Tieng for an afternoon visit. I had worked the morning and we had enough Ravens airborne to cover the rest of the day so I agreed to take the guy for a ride. He had already irritated a few of us by asking if we could tell him something that CIA didn't know so they could do a "gotcha" at the Country Team meeting. We kind of eye-rolled that one.

I flew him around in an O-1 for over two hours, flying low in safe areas, pointing out what happened where and when, and giving a basic tour. When we got back to Long Tieng he said to me, "That ought to good enough for a DFC, don't you think"? I was utterly astounded. My reply was a very terse, "If it were I've have 300 of them." He left on the shuttle.

He apparently thought that having a DFC, however phony, would get him promoted. He later manufactured an absurd "requirement" for a recon version of the T-28 to collect imagery of the "Chinese Road". He flew in the back seat with Don Moody doing the flying. They nearly got zapped and he got himself a DFC. He did not get promoted. It should be mentioned that there was plenty of U-2, SR-71, and satellite imagery of the China Road. Nobody needed any imagery from a T-28.

The use of airpower continued to be split between supply interdiction and troops-in-contact or troop concentration targets. The fast FAC, largely confined to LOC, continued their interdiction efforts. This led to a couple of interesting situations.

CBU 24 was the standard cluster bomb munition carried by fast movers. It was released at about 4000 AGL in a steep dive and spread in a circular pattern some 300 meters across. The slow movers carried a couple of varieties of stream dispensed CBU. This was released in level flight at a fairly low altitude with the bomblets streaming aft from a dispenser which remained on a pylon under the wings. A derivation of CBU 24 had been developed and was stream dispensed by fast movers at fairly low altitude. The bomblets looked like CBU 24 (envision a fluted tennis ball) except that there were 16 hair thin wires that snapped out from the bomblet after it had stopped moving. The wires were probably about eight feet long. If they were disturbed by something passing by, such as a supply porter, and the bomblet rotated a few degrees in response, the bomblet exploded with the same awesome effects as CBU 24. It was supposed to self-destruct after 28 days. I recall its designation

CHAPTER TEN

as CBU 42 but am not sure. It was very expensive and the Air Force didn't want to have us use new and expensive munitions.

It didn't take long for it to dawn on someone in Saigon that this new toy syndrome was not very useful. They might have the munitions but we knew where the supply trails were and had sources frequently observing. We worked a number of CBU 42 drops on trails on the west end of Ban Ban and where Route 7 exited there to the PDJ. We would stream one canister for a kilometer, leave a kilometer open, and stream more CBU. The porters and troops would take considerable casualties, and spend lots of time, getting through the first drop area. Then, finding themselves free of this nasty stuff, they would go charging forward until they hit the next patch.

Another interdiction technique used by the Air Force was to "cut" a road by creating a large enough bomb crater condition so that trucks could not drive around the cratered area because of obstructions alongside the road. Driving through a deep bomb crater is pretty much out of the question. While this had worked in other wars, to some extent, the Vietnamese were extremely resilient at fixing roads and very crafty in various aspects of that activity. The effectiveness of road cuts was far less than those in Saigon would have wished.

Route 61 runs north out of Ban Ban towards Sam Nuea some 45 miles north. A few miles north of Ban Ban there was a section of road that had been built, undoubtedly by the French, by pushing a huge amount of dirt between two hill ridges that reached towards each other. The builders essentially filled a valley gap with dirt and, after allowing for drainage at the bottom, put a two lane dirt road on the top. The sides sloped down from the road at about a 45 degree angle so there was no driving around a large bomb crater. A perfect place for a traditional road cut and that is exactly what was done. We noticed it in October and checked on it periodically. We knew there were supplies brought south on Route 61 and alternatives to the road, while possible, would be nightmarish. Finally, one of us got the clue. One morning there was a set of tire tracks on the north side of the bomb crater and a set of tire tracks on the south edge. The Vietnamese had been filling the crater with dirt as soon as the sun went down, driving over it all night, and then digging the crater out. Someone forgot to brush out the tire tracks. We promptly messaged 7th Air Force but, based on subsequent writings, it appears they didn't believe us.

In the next couple of weeks it started getting obvious, even to me, that my invulnerability cloak was slipping away. I had flown nearly 400 missions as a Raven and had taken no hits, nor had any of the fighters I worked taken any hits. That was very unique at the time since almost everyone else had been hit at least once and a considerable number of fighters had been damaged or shot down.

I was in an O-1 working the eastern end of Ban Ban which was becoming more heavily defended because of the troops and supplies moving through the area. It was a sunny day with scattered puffy clouds and I was fairly high over the target area when I finished briefing the fighters who were moving into their random attack pattern.

I rolled in to mark, picking up the usual amount of speed in the process, and then entered one of the puffy clouds. The O-1 had a "do not exceed" speed of 156 knots but I wasn't paying attention to airspeed while focused on diving through the cloud and waiting to get into clear air where I could fire a rocket. As I came out the bottom of the cloud I heard a severe grinding sound on either side of my head. I looked quickly to either side and saw the wings grinding in their roots. I, foolishly, fired the rocket and glanced at the airspeed. The Birddog was doing 190 knots when I started an extremely gentle dive recovery and

CHAPTER TEN

got rid of the speed by going up vertically. The gunners must have been amazed at seeing an O-1 climb at that rate! The strike against supplies and troops went well but I needed to have a talk with myself, something that did not happen at that point.

The CIA base chief had another special mission for me at a place just south of Route 7 not far from the North Vietnamese border. He showed me a shallow ravine on a 1:50000 a bit west of the village of Nong Het. The ravine was about 400 meters long and perhaps 250 meters wide running roughly north-south. Tomorrow, he said, the area needed to be blanketed with CBU between 1400 and 1700. There was obviously someone of importance in that area but, as usual, I did not know and did not ask.

About 1500 the next day I was in a T-28 and briefed a flight of F-4 that were carrying the standard load of 12 CBU 24 and 48 Mark 82 bombs. The plan was for them to hose the ravine with the CBU first and we would work the bombs later. I fired four rockets to form a box around the ravine and instructed them to fill the box. I got down low over the scattered trees, giving minor corrections, and observed troops running. I was probably about one kilometer from the strike area and was about to say something when I sensed movement above me.

When a CBU canister opened and the CBU started scattering into its circular pattern, some of the bomblets would bang into each other after arming. They would detonate with a white flash as the bomblets descended, leaving a brief trail of fire and white smoke puffs. One of the F-4 had pitched a CBU 24 canister long and it had opened directly above me. In an instant my mind told me that this was the end since if one bomblet out of 670 hit my T-28 it would destroy the airplane and me. I flew through the cloud of bomblets unscathed and they detonated below me seconds later. It took a minute or so for me to regain my composure and half-heartedly work the bombs on the area where I had seen the troops.

It was rice harvesting season and many Hmong farmers behind NVA lines were busy gathering up the mountain rice and piling it into huge stacks that littered the floor of Ban Ban Valley. Each stack weighed about 3000 pounds and, while intended for the farmer, much would go to feed the NVA. This meant they could transport less food and more ammunition into the battle area. It was, certainly, a moral call but the decision was made to destroy rice, or at least what we could see and strike. I worked a few flights of fast movers on rice with mediocre results, mostly because it was difficult to see. On 27 November I worked Firefly 24/25 (two A-1) for 41 minutes while they destroyed 17 tons of rice in addition to causing some secondary explosions and fires. I think all this must have awakened the local gunners.

After working some fast movers on some trucks I returned in my T-28 to the previous area in Ban Ban and made a very low altitude pass on some rice stacks on the south side of the valley, incinerating two stacks with a couple of WP rockets. I stayed low, less than 100 feet, and circled around for another pass on the same area. That was not a smart thing to do but being smart was fading away. The second pass burned up a couple of more stacks. I circled around once again and came in for another couple of low altitude shots. At about my 1130 position, slightly left of straight ahead, I saw the muzzle flash of what my brain instantly told me was 12.7 mm. One round hit a section of fuselage frame, ricocheted, and hit the throttle quadrant just below my left hand. It had to have been a defective round or it would have done more damage, but it was enough to give me a wake-up call. I notified Cricket that I was hit and headed back to Long Tieng since there might be more damage.

CHAPTER TEN

The next day I was over Ban Ban in an O-1 in the same area, at a reasonable altitude, late in the afternoon. A couple of A-1 Sandy, rescue helicopter escorts, had reached the end of their orbit time and asked if I had anything they could dump their "soft load" (napalm, rockets, WP bombs, CBU) on. I told them about the 12.7, whose location was almost beneath me, and was about to mark when the flash of 12.7 streamed out of the tree shadows. The Sandy flight said to forget the mark, they had him – and they did.

On 29 November, in a T-28, I worked a couple of sets of fighters late in the afternoon, after working several more sets earlier while flying an O-1. The late afternoon strikes were close to the Vietnamese border so I decided to go trolling for NVA troops before heading home. There was a thin deck of cloud a few thousand feet above the terrain as I flew about six miles into North Vietnam while looking for any signs of troop formations. On my left, a few miles away, I saw movement and then confirmed a troop formation hiking up a road towards the Lao border.

I gradually turned until I was headed about 20 degrees east of them and simultaneously started a slow descent, leaving engine power untouched in an effort to not alert them. When they were off my left wing and about a thousand feet below me, I armed up the guns, pushed up the power, and rolled inverted into a dive. The idea was to pick up as much speed as possible and then start climbing the road where the troop formation was moving west. They heard me coming and dived into the ditches on either side of the road of the dusty dirt road. I picked the ditch on the left and started hosing them with two second bursts of .50 caliber while no more than 50 feet above them. While I was certainly doing plenty of damage to the troops in the left ditch, I had completely forgotten about the troops in the right ditch. My T-28 canopy was suddenly enveloped in green AK-47 tracer fire from the right. An instantaneous glance to the right revealed scores of troops, most standing, blazing away at me. I was starting to run out of airspeed so this, I figured, was a good time to leave.

I pulled up very steeply at full power and entered the gray-blue cloud deck just as I reached stall speed and nosed over, safe. Gradually picking up speed, I edged up in the clouds to a fading blue sky above and headed home. The view was there was unbelievable. The cloud deck was absolutely flat on top, and golden from the setting sun. I inched the T-28 down until that perfectly flat deck was even with the lower edge of my canopy giving me the illusion that I was no longer in an airplane but some kind of bubble with a prop in front of it. I made a few turns just to look at where the airplane had left a wake, much like a boat. Pulling my pipe out of a lower flight suit pocket, I stuffed it with tobacco and tried to light it, to no avail. My hands had been getting shaky but this was so bad I couldn't light my pipe no matter what I did. I got the message, my time as a Raven was over. I played with the clouds some more and then dropped down to land in a darkening valley that was home.

That evening I told Joe Potter where I thought I was on all this and he, having been through this before, agreed. The next morning I flew to Vientiane to talk to Andy Patten, feeling somehow guilty. Andy, I knew, had been watching me for a while and this was no surprise to him. He suggested I quit now, that day. I countered with "one more day".

When I returned to Long Tieng I switched over to a T-28, did some sightseeing, and worked a couple of flights of A-1. On my second sortie on 1 December there was a perfect example of why we were so often so effective. One of the case officers that worked out of LS-46 was on a hill overlooking a village that had just been occupied by the NVA, the villagers fleeing up the hill to where the case officer watched. This was well east of the town of Xieng Khoung and well south of Route 7. A modest

CHAPTER TEN

river was a bit farther south, gently flowing through jungle valleys to join the labyrinth of waterways that eventually reached the Mekong.

Two A-1, Zorro 50 and 51, checked in and I, following the guidance of the case officer, directed the hammering of the NVA. The case officer, sounding a bit excited, asked if they had any ordnance left since there was what looked like two companies of NVA wading across the river. Zorro had stream dispensed anti-personnel CBU remaining so I had them drop behind me in an extended trail position as I headed for the river, less than a mile away. I told Zorro what was going on and asked them to start dispensing CBU where I rocked my wings. This would be guesswork but worth the try.

There was a real crowd stretched across the river, slowed down by the waist deep water. I was at perhaps five hundred feet when I rocked my wings and a few seconds later Zorro started dumping CBU. The A-1 continued on their way as I climbed and started a big circle to cross where the troops had been. The slow moving river speckled with sunlight and the crowd of troops seemed much smaller. Then I could see numerous darker objects slowly floating away amidst a wide reddish cloud in the water. I was done.

EPILOGUE

I had a couple of weeks left at Long Tieng before I departed to my next duty station, Hurlburt Field, Florida as an O-1 instructor pilot. This was a dead end assignment, something many Ravens got, but I had been so involved at Long Tieng that I had not considered the implications until this point. Many Ravens had been getting bad assignments and it is difficult to recover from that since one bad one often leads to another. Major General Robert Dixon, later commander of Tactical Air Command, had visited Long Tieng, while I was on leave, and acknowledged that bad follow-on assignments were too much the norm for Ravens and said he would look into it. The then-chief of rated assignments at the Air Force Personnel Center, recently told me that there was no USAF assignment policy working against Ravens. That is a bit hard to believe given the conversations that occurred between Ravens and some of the rated-personnel types. In any event, that was the hand I was dealt and it was probably a better place than being dropped into the rigidity of the training command environment, or some such place. I was eventually rescued from Hurlburt Field by a Lieutenant General who had been in my father's pilot training class. This involved another combat tour, this in the RF-4, which led to a series of interesting assignments in intelligence.

In the meantime, I ferried aircraft back and forth to Udorn, slept in, had a couple of adventures, ate good meals prepared by the new cooks, read a lot, and thought about where I had been, what I had experienced, and what I had learned.

Gia Nghia seemed a much more distant past than could be explained by any chronological measurement. It had been a useful place to learn the basics and examine, based on daily experience, where we were, or were not, going in a major national effort at least as defined in that part of Vietnam at that time. Life at Long Tieng had been a whole new and different experience in many ways.

The CIA had a defined mission in Laos and we were a critical part of executing that mission. In that process we were provided with information, intelligence, and insights into the military and political behavior of the enemy. This level of support permitted us to perceive and take advantage of enemy weaknesses, doing much to enable the CIA to accomplish much of the task assigned to them by the President of the United States.

Operating as a Raven was an incredibly tense and demanding experience that forced a great deal of self-examination during the process of directing massive amounts of firepower in an extremely lethal environment. One discovered personal boundaries and limitations in a fashion that would have an indelible effect on future approaches to difficult situations. Finally, this experience tended to provoke questions, said or unsaid, about the effectiveness and utility of any current means of doing business, including the business of setting policy goals and conducting warfare. Every situation is formed by many different variables that must be understood before engaging in attempting a useful change to that environment. Reality demands flexibility if success is a desired outcome.

EPILOGUE

On the evening of 16 December Bob Dunbar, Al Daines, and I were the honored guests at a traditional baci ceremony at Vang Pao's house. We sat on pillows while a long line of Hmong went past, on their knees the last few feet of the process, and we exchanged greetings using the wye position until my arms hurt. At the end, Vang Pao brought out a bottle of excellent cognac and we all had a shot, except Al Daines who was a Morman. He was hoping to be offered a shot which he would take as a mandatory political and social obligation. Vang Pao, however, said that he understood Al's religion did not permit drinking so he passed him by. Al was very disappointed.

Almost every problem situation in human endeavor requires a close examination to find an underlying cause so that one or more appropriate means can be selected to achieve change. Warfare is no different. There is almost never a single answer or fix and clinging to one in spite of reality is a formula for disaster.

When I flew south from Long Tieng in a T-28 for the last time, I was departing a physical place but keeping an unforgettable part of my life that influenced me forever.